THE BRITISH BOOK OF
RAILWAYS

Copy Editor: William J. Howell
Art Editor: Deborah Miles
Design: Mark Holt

ACKNOWLEDGEMENTS
Much of the material in this book appeared originally in the
partwork, HISTORY OF RAILWAYS, and its sequel, GREAT
TRAINS, and I am indebted to E. L. Cornwell, the editor of
those publications, for making my editorial task on the book easier
than it might otherwise have been. My special thanks go to
Richard Hosburn for his skill in condensing and rewriting
material for the book and to Eileen Murphy for her administrative
help. Finally, I wish to express my appreciation to all those
whose textual and illustrative contributions appear in this book
M.O.

This edition published in 1978 by
New English Library Limited,
Barnard's Inn,
Holborn,
London EC1N 2JR,
England

Set in 11/12pt Monotype Plantin by South Bucks Typesetters
Limited
Printed by Fratelli Spada, Ciampino, Rome, Italy

45003575 1

THE BRITISH BOOK OF RAILWAYS

EDITED BY MICHAEL OLDHAM

NEW ENGLISH LIBRARY

TIMES MIRROR

Contents

Facing page: Keighley & Worth Valley Railway's American-built 0-6-0T locomotive No 72, 'Tornado', one of several bought by the Southern Railway for work in Southampton docks during the Second World War. J. BENTON HARRIS

Early Locomotives

Steam engines had come to be widely used in major industries in Britain by the end of the eighteenth century. In factories they were used to drive elaborate and complex machinery, whilst in the mines they operated lifts and water-pumps. But these cumbersome devices were so enormous and weighty that they would never have moved about on wheels under their own power. The usual procedure was to erect them and then build a giant shed around them. It was not until 1804 that the first railway locomotive was built by engineer and designer Richard Trevithick.

Following the invention by James Watt of the steam engine, Trevithick had experimented for some time with the use of steam pressure as high as 25lbs per square inch. Before long he found that a modified version of one of his stationary engines was powerful enough to run along on wheels under its own drive. The idea of a self-propelling engine had been shown to be possible, but the experimental vehicle was soon taken off its wheels and installed in a foundry.

Trevithick's second locomotive was displayed on a circular demonstration track in London four years later and received considerable attention from the public. In 1812 the

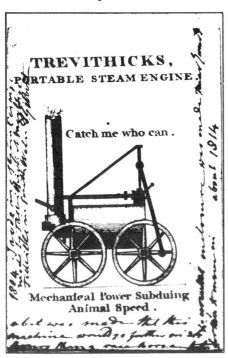

Middleton Railway near Leeds bought four machines which were modified versions of Trevithick's design, and these ran successfully for over twenty years. Just one year later the Wylam Railway near Newcastle adopted three steam locomotives built on similar lines, one of which was the legendary *Puffing Billy*, and they remained in service for almost fifty years.

Whilst the Wylam Railway had chosen Trevithick's own design for the track, the Middleton Railway's Manager, John Blenkinsop, did not believe that the smooth iron wheel would be able to grip a smooth iron rail sufficiently. As a result, the engines on the Middleton lines used a toothed cog-like wheel which engaged with a pinion cast onto the outer edge of one rail.

The problem of track-efficiency caused much thought among the engineers of the time. It was natural that they should be concerned, for horse-drawn wagons in the mines had long demonstrated the difficulty of braking in wet weather on steep descents laid with iron rails. Although the solution developed by Blenkinsop on the Middleton Railway was certainly effective, it was expensive. Other experimenters tried locomotives which winched themselves along on a chain, or lumbered along on mechanical legs.

William Hedley, the engineer of the Wylam Railway, built a wagon whose wheels were turned by a crank-system operated by a crew of men working on top. By using ballast weights, Hedley installed an iron wheel which *did* have enough bite on the rail to draw a useful load without any other assistance. Like Blenkinsop, he followed Trevithick's designs, but with his own improvements, and he retained Trevithick's effective boiler.

Thanks largely to the efforts of another engineer these advances were not put aside and neglected, for the years between 1814 and 1826 were hard for small businesses, and many enterprising experiments had been abandoned through lack of funds. During this time, George Stephenson was the only man in Britain who built locomotives. Born near Wylam, in the Tyne Valley, Stephenson had studied the operation of the engines and machinery in the local collieries and improved their efficiency with his own designs.

Among Stephenson's other achievements was his safety lamp produced for use in the coal-mines following a series of pit explosions. Many argue that in some ways it was preferable to the lamp designed at the same time by Sir Humphry Davy, which later became universally used. The leaders of local large industries had appointed Stephenson to supervise the working of all their machinery, and the sight of the locomotives on the nearby Wylam Railway sparked off much interest. The price of horse fodder had soared, and local industrialists disliked the idea of a neighbouring competitor seeming to be more progressive than they.

As a result, they instructed Stephenson to build a locomotive for their Killingworth Railway. Stephenson's first machine, the *Blucher*, took to the rails in 1814. In many ways it was a close copy of the Middleton engines, though without the rack drive. Although he was not an adventurous engineer by nature, Stephenson was a sound worker, and was quite prepared to take small experimental steps which gradually built up to considerable improvements. In his design, Stephenson had copied an earlier and rather inefficient boiler arrangement which had only a single large fire-tube set inside the boiler barrel. So although Stephenson had brought about many improvements on older designs, the major weakness of his first model was in its boiler system.

After further experiments, Stephenson decided to do away with the expensive and awkward train of gears which provided the transmission of power to the wheels, and to use instead a sprocket chain invented by himself for this purpose. He was also responsible for the development of improved cast-iron rails and wheels, as well as the first steel springs strong enough to carry weights of several tons or more. Through the Killingworth Railway, locomotives gradually became more and more familiar until, by the mid-1820s, there was serious talk of building a national network of steam railways.

In 1821 George Stephenson was appointed engineer of the Stockton & Darlington Railway, and laid out its main line for twenty-two miles from Shildon to Stockton – the longest run that steam locomotives had yet undertaken. Earlier railway systems had been developed largely by the mines and other industries to carry out a limited function for the companies which had built them. Understandably enough, the opening of the Stockton & Darlington line in 1825, the first railway to operate public traffic, proved to be a topic of widespread interest. Although support for this ambitious experiment in steam power came immediately, there were many people who were not so enthusiastic. The noise, the volumes of smoke, and the risk of fire from the hot coals thrown out onto the line were all subjects of complaint by local landowners, and

eventually legal steps were taken to try to stop this public 'nuisance'.

These events were soon followed by a widespread reaction to railways from environmentalists and sceptics who saw the railways as a grave threat to the standard of living. There were others who dismissed the whole idea of commercial railways as an idle fantasy, arguing that they would never be economical enough to pay their own way. Since the Stockton & Darlington line was worked by both steam power and horse-drawn wagons, it provided a good testing-ground to decide the arguments. As early as 1827 the directors of the railways were claiming that their steam engines were saving up to thirty per cent in costs compared with the traditional horse-drawn trains. Here at last was proof that, whatever the problems ahead – and there were many – at least there was some kind of a future for the steam railways.

A year after the opening of the Stockton & Darlington line, the thirty-mile long Liverpool & Manchester Railway was started. This was the world's first line intended to form the main link for inter-city traffic of all kinds. The Liverpool & Manchester had double track throughout, and was a much greater undertaking than the Stockton & Darlington. Horse-drawn trains were never considered for the new line, and the directors put all their efforts into backing steam locomotives.

In 1829 the Liverpool & Man-chester directors made it known that they were offering a substantial prize to the builder of the best locomotive, and arranged for a contest to be held that autumn on a completed section of the line at Rainhill. Certain conditions were set for designers enter-ing the contest: the engine was not to weigh more than four and a half tons (if four-wheeled) or six tons (if six-wheeled), and it should use steam at a pressure of not more than 50lb per square inch. There were restric-tions on the amount of smoke which could be emitted, and the engine had to haul a load of three times its own weight at 10 mph for a total of thirty miles.

The rules were certainly tough and deterred some of the less accomplish-ed engineers in this field, although one determined gentleman entered a horse-driven wagon which had the horse enclosed in it running on a treadmill! Many inventors who had given notice that they intended to compete, met with unexpected prob-lems and failed to reach the starting line. In the end there were only three serious contestants.

Firstly there was Timothy Hack-worth's *Sanspareil*, which was a smaller four-wheeled version of the standard Stockton & Darlington loco-motive. Next there was Braithwaite and Ericsson's *Novelty*, a light-weight and unconventional machine, and thirdly, Robert Stephenson's *Rocket*. Robert was the son of George Stephenson, and his design made it clear that he had learned much from his father's pioneering work.

The *Sanspareil* had been built in a great hurry, and in the end it failed to meet the terms of the contest. It was rather overweight, was wasteful of fuel and had a leaky boiler. It was surprising in many ways that it ran at all, for the design contained many weaknesses which, with a little more time, might have been overcome by Hackworth. The *Novelty*, although the favourite with the crowd, was not up to the heavy work demanded

of it. Despite lapping the course at over 30 mph, looking impressive with its glittering paint and polish, the *Novelty* soon developed trouble in its boiler. Suddenly, with a loud bang, it came to a halt and had to be pushed clear of the track.

The *Rocket* had also been built in considerable haste, but showed that its designer had given much careful thought to the project. It had an entirely new kind of boiler which used many small tubes to convey heat to the water, instead of one large tube. The cylinders were located in a different way to enable them to drive the wheels directly, and much expense and weight were saved by using only one pair of driving wheels. The *Rocket* was more simple and yet more efficient than any of the earlier locomotive designs, and it romped home with the prize.

Having fulfilled the terms of the contest, Stephenson put his machine through severe testing on the last run, and almost matched the impressive speed recorded by the *Novelty*. Then he picked up a coachload of passengers and steamed them smartly up and down a nearby incline, proving beyond doubt that his engine was not only fast but remarkably powerful too. Thus the *Rocket* had demonstrated to engineering experts and the public alike that steam locomotion had a responsible part to play in the future of transport.

Over the years, however, even the *Rocket* found itself outdated and came to a halt at the Science Museum in London.

The great contribution made in the field of locomotives by the younger Stephenson was not to come to an end with the *Rocket*. Exactly a year after the Rainhill contest had taken place, the Liverpool & Manchester Railway was opened to public traffic, and by this time Robert Stephenson's small works in Newcastle had built seven or eight more engines, improving on the original *Rocket* design as the work progressed. The tremendous public interest awakened by the opening of the new line brought a flurry of activity in engineering circles. The trains were carrying crowds of eager and excited passengers and running to a strict timetable, and train-weights began to be increased beyond all previous forecasts.

Stephenson had evolved a standard boiler design for his engines, and this gradually came to be fitted to most steam locomotives from that time onwards. New and improved frames were built to carry the increasing weight of the engines, which themselves were becoming larger and more powerful. The final engines of the Rocket class weighed almost eight tons, but Stephenson dropped this design in 1830 in favour of the Planet type.

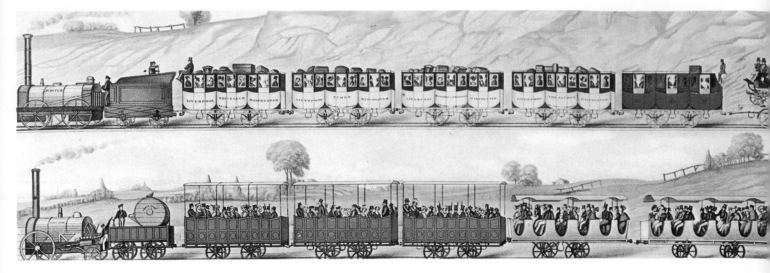

The Planets retained all the advances which Stephenson had made with the Rockets, but the cylinders were moved from the rear of the engine to a forward position. This led to the building of a great number of similar engines by a variety of firms, and before long it became a standard practice to position the cylinders at the front-end of the engine. These locomotives were used exclusively on the London & Birmingham Railway for some years after its opening in 1838, and were exported to several countries overseas, including the United States.

As the years went by and the volume of traffic began to increase rapidly, the early railway companies found themselves faced with further problems. Firstly there was a need for the engines to be powerful enough to haul their giant loads, and secondly the track was in danger of becoming outdated. With four-wheeled locomotives weighing about ten tons running up and down the lines, the cost of maintaining the track was becoming high. The solution was to have larger engines with six wheels.

In 1833 Stephenson brought out the Patentee class, which was basically a Planet engine with an additional pair of carrying wheels at the rear. The opportunities for further variations on this theme were not neglected, and before long the London & Manchester had introduced a number of Patentees with four wheels coupled. These powerful giants were given descriptive names like *Samson* and *Elephant*, and one of them – the *Lion* of 1838 – still survives as a working museum-piece.

One Patentee-type engine with all six wheels coupled was built for the Leicester & Swannington Railway in 1834. This locomotive weighed seventeen tons and was in every important respect the forerunner of the standard British goods engine, the inside-cylinder 0-6-0, which was built in various shapes and sizes and in enormous numbers over the next 110 years.

It is hard to believe that this significant design had emerged only five years after Robert Stephenson's *Rocket* had first steamed out before eager crowds at Rainhill. The impact of Stephenson's careful and competent designs had been so great that up-and-coming engineers all over the country put their minds to working in the new field of steam locomotion, and the result proved to be one of the most remarkable achievements of modern technology. The only changes made on Britain's railways between Stephenson's day and the early 1950s were little more than minor improvements: the groundwork for a national railway system had been carried out by a handful of brilliant and dedicated men in only a few years. It was their persistent belief in the new concept of steam locomotion that brought the railways as we know them today into existence.

Top: Aquatints by J. Shaw showing trains at work on the Liverpool & Manchester Railway. NATIONAL RAILWAY MUSEUM, YORK (B. SHARPE)

Below: One of Stephenson's Patentee 2-2-2 locomotives as built from about 1834 to 1850. SCIENCE MUSEUM, LONDON

The Story of Railway Tickets

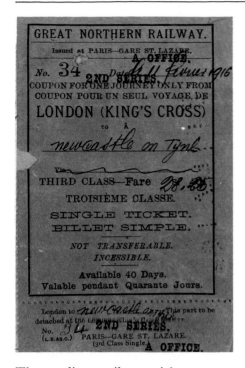

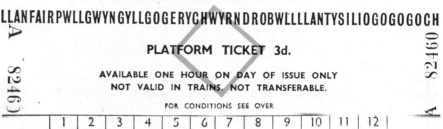

Far left: A ticket issued at Gare St Lazare, Paris, for a journey in Britain in 1916. Left: A child's first-class ticket of the Liverpool Overhead Railway. Below: a long ticket for the long-named station in Anglesey. J. E. SHELBOURN

The earliest railway tickets were small slips of paper cut from a book by the station clerk, who filled in all the travel details by hand. This slow, laborious practice had become a nuisance by the 1830s because of the number of passengers who were travelling and the delay in writing the tickets, and the railway companies began to look for a speedier process.

It was found by a station clerk named Thomas Edmondson who invented the earliest printed tickets and patented other equipment such as dating machines and clippers. These tickets were sold over the counter for cash, and the idea spread rapidly until it became a standard procedure for almost all railway companies the world over.

Colour has always been important in railway tickets, and from the earliest days colour has been used to distinguish one kind of ticket from another. Most companies have kept to the same pattern, issuing white tickets for first-class, pink or blue for second-class and green or beige for third-class travellers. There were exceptions to the rule, when multi-coloured tickets were used for some classes of traffic and striped tickets for others. For a time the Great Eastern Railway issued tickets of one colour for the outward journeys and a different colour for the return di-

rection – a useful aid to the busy ticket collector. Today, British Rail tickets for first-class travel are white, and green means second-class – an unfortunate clash with the colours on the Continent, where, by international agreement, first-class tickets are green.

On most railway systems, reductions are made for children below a certain age, for whom the cost of the fare is normally cut by half. The different forms of reduced-cost travel means that there is still a great variety in the designs of tickets today. Cheap fares are offered in three main classes, the commonest being the off-peak or cheap return fares. Another category is the special-rate tickets issued as a privilege for certain kinds of people such as railway staff and groups on excursions. Thirdly, there are tickets which cover full travel by more than one means – perhaps by rail and bus, or rail and ship. Platform tickets are used everywhere of course, but they are not used for any form of rail travel.

The use of machines for issuing tickets dates back as far as 1900 when the French Paris Métropolitain took up the idea. The London Underground soon followed the example, although the devices used were primitive by modern standards. In 1907 a new German machine which could

print tickets from a selection of stored plates was tried on main-line railway routes in Prussia, and before long spread all over Europe.

More recent advances in techniques for inspecting tickets include the coded message system. This enables modern railways to install machines which can 'read' specially-printed magnetic strips in the ticket which record the date, time and fare. If the ticket is out of date or not valid for some other reason, it is refused by the machine and the passenger must pay the full fare. The London Underground has pioneered this field on a large scale, setting up automatic barriers and complicated vending machines at many important stations, but there are still problems involved, and tickets are still issued and collected by hand. Some time has yet to pass before these methods become reliable and efficient enough for the entire ticket process to be handled automatically. Other new ideas are being studied and tried out by various railway companies throughout the world, one of which is the ambitious plan to run a fully automatic train service with special carriages which will allow the passenger on board only after the correct ticket has been inserted into a slot machine mounted inside the train.

The London & North Eastern Railway

The London & North Eastern Railway's roots go back to George Stephenson and the world's first public railway. Its largest, wealthiest and most influential constituent company – the North Eastern – was itself descended from the Stockton & Darlington, which opened in 1825. The North Eastern had almost entire control of the North and East Ridings of Yorkshire, the counties of Durham and Northumberland, and running powers right through the north of Britain to Edinburgh. In 1922 it swallowed its rival, the Hull & Barnsley, and finished up with more than 5,400 miles of track.

The next largest company inside the LNER was the Great Northern, which operated in an area just south of the North Eastern. The Great Northern did not come into existence until 1846, and from the start set Yorkshire as its target, using King's Cross as its terminus from

LNER

ON
3ʳᵈ JULY 1938
THIS LOCOMOTIVE
ATTAINED A
WORLD SPEED RECORD
FOR STEAM TRACTION
OF 126
MILES PER HOUR

1852. The two other English 'greats' taken in during the Grouping of the railways in 1923 were the Great Central and the Great Eastern.

In Scotland the LNER absorbed the North British, the largest Scottish railway, and the Great North of Scotland. Like the Great Eastern, the Great North railway was a royal line, in that its branch from Aberdeen to Ballater served the royal residence of Balmoral. The LNER shared two lines with the LMS, the Cheshire Lines Committee (partly in Cheshire) and the Midland & Great Northern.

In some ways the formation of the LNER smoothed out the often uneasy alliances between companies which had become established as the East Coast route. The East Coast companies, the Great Northern, North Eastern and North British, provided a fast service between London and Edinburgh. The addi-

tion of the Great Central, Great Eastern and Great North of Scotland companies was complementary. Fortunately the merging of these various organisations within the LNER proved to be a trouble-free operation, and the LNER was the host for the Railway Centenary celebrations of 1925.

As part of the celebrations, engines ranging from the ancient Hetton Colliery locomotive of 1822 to an ex-Gresley Pacific, a Southern King Arthur and, above all, a Great Western Castle, ran over the Stockton & Darlington route in the presence of royalty. That year, too, there were the famous exchanges between the LNER and the Great Western, when the Pacific locomotives were tried out against the Castles.

Competition between the companies of the East Coast route and its rivals on the West Coast had continued over the years, but it was stepped up when the LMS, with its new Royal Scot-class locomotives, began to run non-stop between London and Carlisle in 1928. In retaliation the LNER brought the new *Flying Scotsman* into service, with the longest non-stop run in the world, 393 miles, between London and Edinburgh made possible by the use of a corridor tender, which enabled locomotive crews to change over during the journey without the train having to stop.

By 1935 streamlining had come into vogue with the *Silver Jubilee* train, which reached Newcastle within four hours from London. So successful was the train that a further flyer, the *Coronation*, began to run in 1937. The *Coronation* took the speed record of the day by being booked to run between King's Cross and York at an average speed of 71.9 mph. The next stop, Edinburgh, was reached six hours after the departure from London. By the following year the *West Riding Limited* was operating out of King's Cross to Bradford

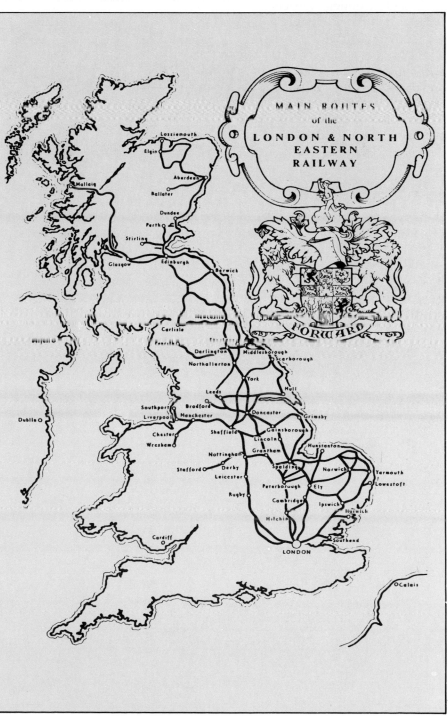

Top, right: A GER J15 0-6-0 of 1883 vintage, preserved at Sheringham by the Midland & Great Northern Joint Preservation Society. V. C. K. ALLEN

Right: Map of the principal lines of the LNER at Grouping in 1923.

with a timing which was not bettered until 1966 with the modern Deltic diesel engines.

The LNER was fortunate in having amongst its employees Nigel Gresley, whose locomotives became world famous. Gresley's policy was to use the best of the old designs and add his own improvements, and there can be little doubt that it was a successful approach. Of all British express engines at the time of the Grouping, his A3-class Pacifics and the A1 *Flying Scotsman* were not only the most handsome, but also the finest examples of what was best in express steam locomotives.

In 1925 the LNER obtained a 2-8-8-2 Garratt engine, built to Gresley's design by Beyer Peacock & Co. It was the most powerful steam engine ever to be built for use in Britain, and was designed to run on the steep seven-mile slope on the old Great Central route from Wath to Lancashire via the Woodhead tunnel. In 1935 Gresley's A4 Pacific was completed, and on trial runs twice reached the record speed of $112\frac{1}{2}$ mph. By 1938, thirty-five had been built and were in regular service; of them No 4468 Mallard attained the world speed record for steam of 126 mph. Most LNER engines were either built at the old Great Northern works at Doncaster, or the North Eastern shops at Darlington.

Although the LNER had not been diesel-minded in its planning, it had turned its thoughts towards electrification. It inherited the Tyneside electric trains from the North Eastern and joined with the LMS in the electrification of the joint Manchester South Junction and Altrincham line. In London the company worked with the London Passenger Transport Board in the electrification of some of its suburban routes. There was also an ambitious plan to electrify the section from Manchester to Sheffield, but this could not be completed until the long Woodhead tunnel was rebuilt, and the project was not finished until after nationalisation of the railways.

The LNER spread its non-railway activities widely, and owned a considerable number of ships, besides the largest number of docks and harbours of any of the railway companies. Most were on the Tyne, Tees and Humber, though to travel-

lers Harwich was no doubt the best known. Passenger steamships left Grimsby for Hamburg, Harwich for Holland and Hull for Germany, France and Belgium. In Scotland the company also operated a delightful fleet of ex-North British Railway paddle steamers.

Hotels were a profitable investment, and the LNER inherited a large number of them from its constituent companies. Among the most notable were those at Liverpool Street, London, and at Edinburgh. The Great Central put up a huge building at Marylebone, which is now the headquarters of the British Railways Board, and most towns of a certain size had their railway hotel if they lay on a LNER route.

Like other railways, the LNER was slow to realise the extent of the threat presented by road transport. Efforts were made during the 1930s to combine with the other railway

companies in calling for a change in the laws affecting railway freight handling, but little was achieved. The Transport Act of 1953 secured some improvements, but by then it was too late, and the advantages of motorised transport put the railways firmly in second place.

After the Second World War it was clear that either the railways would need to be given a massive subsidy, or that they should be nationalised outright. The latter course was chosen and the LNER disappeared on 31 December 1947. Unfortunately, from its shareholders' point of view, it had not been a great success. In fact, the LNER had the worst financial record of the big four companies, but it is to the LNER's credit that it was able to perform as well as it did. It had some first-class railway officers too, and many of them reached the highest ranks in the new British Railways' organisation.

Left: The Gresley streamlined A4 Pacific 'Mallard', preserved at the National Railway Museum, York.

Right: A BR 3,300hp Deltic diesel-electric locomotive, photographed at King's Cross, engaged in maintaining the tradition of fast passenger services on the East Coast route. G. P. COOPER

Below: A W. Worsdell 0-6-0T – a NER shunter standardised by British Railways for the North Eastern Region, at work as a Newcastle pilot. J. ADAMS

The Festiniog Railway

The slate-mining town of Blaenau Ffestiniog is thirteen miles from the sea and the harbour at Porthmadog, and in pre-railway days the slate was carried by mules over rough tracks from the mines and quarries to the river Dwyryd near Maentwrog. From there it was taken by barge to sea-going vessels, and the whole process was slow and cumbersome.

By the 1830s the generally accepted solution to most transport problems was to build a railway, and before long a railway was constructed from Blaenau Ffestiniog to Porthmadog. An incredible railway it was, too, even allowing for the fact that its gauge of less than two feet was

under half the size of the standard gauge of that time.

For the first mile out of Porthmadog the line runs almost dead level, but, turning inland at Boston Lodge, it begins to climb a steady slope running for twelve miles. Hugging the mountainside, the line twists and turns so much that at one point, Tan y Bwlch, the up-train actually turns to face Porthmadog again, though it is still travelling to Blaenau Ffestiniog! The position of the railway high over the very beautiful Vale of Ffestiniog is one of the attractions for the thousands of visitors who use the line.

When it was first opened in 1836, the railway was operated by loaded wagons which were allowed to roll down to the coast by gravity. On arrival they were unloaded and then dragged up to the top again by horses. Although quite usual on Britain's standard-gauge lines at this time, steam locomotives were considered an impossible means of transport on such a narrow track. The critics were silenced, however, when four locomotives were built in 1863.

Although hardly conventional, the four machines, and two more of a slightly 'hotted up' version which came later, were quite normal compared with what followed next. *Little Wonder*, which arrived in 1869, was

Left: The Fairlie 0-4-4-0T No 3 'Earl of Merioneth' at Porthmadog. M. POPE

Right: Volunteers hard at work building the Festiniog 'deviation' line at Dduallt. N. F. GURLEY

Below, left: Hunslets' 0-4-0ST 'Blanche' approaching Campbell's Platform, with the mountain Moelwyn Bach (Little Moelwyn) in the background. N. F. GURLEY

Below, centre: Double Fairlie locomotives 'Merddyn Emrys' and 'Earl of Merioneth'. P. B. WHITEHOUSE

Below, right: 'Merddyn Emrys', a Fairlie 0-4-4-0T, taking a train out of Porthmadog, Easter 1972. C. M. WHITEHOUSE

the first of the famous double engines to make its appearance on the Festiniog Railway. Basically it consisted of two locos back to back with a centre cab, so that it could be run in either direction with an enormous source of power.

These steam locos were a very rare breed, and of the two surviving engines, the *Livingston Thomas* is being preserved in its original form as a museum piece. In 1872 two iron-framed bogie coaches were built to cater for the increasing passenger traffic, and they were certainly the first such designs ever built in Britain. But in spite of its success, the long-term prosperity really depended on the slate industry, and when, after 1900, slates began to be replaced by roofing tiles for the majority of new buildings, the railway soon found business dwindling.

To a certain extent the fall in traffic was offset by the growth of tourism in the area, and the railway struggled on until the outbreak of war in 1939, when all holiday traffic ceased and only three slate trains a week came through the line. In 1946

it was closed altogether, and that was very nearly the end of it.

Although many enthusiasts and well-wishers expressed their sorrow at the closure, it was not until 1951 that the Festiniog Railway Society was formed in Bristol. The body of this society now acts as a special kind of supporters' association to the operating company. Renovation proved to be a big task, for it was found that bushes and even trees had grown up in between the rails. But in 1955 a petrol locomotive and two coaches were run on the one-mile section from Porthmadog to Boston Lodge. *Prince*, one of the original 1863 engines, was soon back in service too, and the following year the route was re-opened for a further mile. To maintain the eleven locomotives, twenty-five coaches and hundred or so goods wagons which now operate the line, there is a large workshop at Boston Lodge, claimed to be the largest and best-equipped of its type in Britain.

Left: 'Earl of Merioneth' getting attention at Boston Lodge in August 1970. J. HUNT

Below: The badge of the Festiniog Railway.

Bottom: Head-on view of 2-6-2T 'Mountaineer'; built in 1916 by Alco, USA. N. F. GURLEY

Whistles in the Night

A steam locomotive's whistle sounding across a prairie or echoing between the buildings of a town was enough in itself to convey all the flavour, bustle and character of a steam railway. Everybody knew the whistle, yet even today there is un-

were quick to see the value of the safety-valve as a warning device to scare animals off the tracks, and before long the device was used for that purpose. Although there is no firm evidence to support this claim, it is known that the first steam

more elaborate form of making a noise by blowing air across the top of a bottle. The pioneers of steam whistle design began to enlarge on this idea, and before long all kinds of variations were put into use.

Then came the diesel engine, and

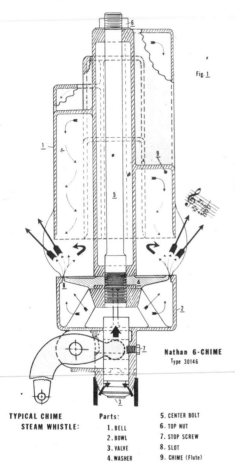

TYPICAL CHIME STEAM WHISTLE:

Parts:
1. BELL
2. BOWL
3. VALVE
4. WASHER
5. CENTER BOLT
6. TOP NUT
7. STOP SCREW
8. SLOT
9. CHIME (Flute)

Nathan 6-CHIME Type 30146

Far left: How it works – a typical chime steam whistle.

Above: The locomotive 'Samson' – the first ever to be fitted with a steam whistle – on the Leicester & Swannington Railway, 1835: from a painting by C. Hamilton Ellis. NATIONAL RAILWAY MUSEUM, YORK (B. SHARPE)

Left: Nathan P-series horn designed to reduce air consumption while retaining the notes of the M-5, on a rare Alco (USA) T6 locomotive of Norfolk & Western Railway. D. H. ELLSWORTH

certainty about its origin.

Some people say that a Mr Whistler invented a single-note device for a steam locomotive that was said to make 'a very high-pitched screech' when sounded. The device was supposed to have been named after its inventor, but there is little evidence to support the tale, and the word 'whistle' existed long before Mr Whistler's time.

Another story concerns an early British locomotive firm during the 1840s which developed a safety-valve designed to release pressure from a locomotive steam boiler to avoid explosion. The device was like a long tin whistle, and the escaping steam was believed to give out a long, shrill, wailing noise. British railroaders

whistles were a product of British locomotive builders, and were introduced to the United States with British-made railroad locomotives. All known whistles at that time were single-noters and the Americans called them 'hooters'.

The story of the chime, or multiple-tone steam whistle, is well recorded and known to be true. The Brooks Locomotive Works of Dunkirk, New York, was one of America's first successful locomotive firms, and is believed to have produced the whistle which one day would be duplicated on every railroad company in Mexico, the USA and Canada -- the melodious chime steam whistle.

A steam whistle operates in the same way as a pipe organ, and is a

with it change. Although diesels were put into passenger service, and consequently had steam-generating equipment for heating, they could not provide enough steam pressure to work even the smallest kind of steam whistle. A type of air-horn, rather like a trumpet, was developed for these trains, and when the diesel went into main-line service in the 1940s, the single-note bleat of its horn began to challenge the chime steam whistle as the familiar tune of the railroad.

Out on the highway, too, more and more trucks were beginning to carry air-horns. But there was a dangerous similarity between the sound of one air-horn and another. Truck drivers, on hearing the sound of an approaching air-horn, thought it was just another truck, and all too often found themselves crossing railroad tracks right in front of a speeding diesel train. Trains didn't sound like trains any more, and something had to be done.

Robert Swanson, a well-known engineer of his time, well experienced in making many fine steam whistles, studied the theory of music, and set about developing an air-horn which would sound more like the old-fashioned steam whistle than the popular single-note horn. The result was the Swanson M-5, which many people still consider to be the finest-sounding chime air-horn ever invented. Swanson horns are now made by the Airchime Manufacturing Company of Vancouver in Canada, and are almost exclusively used in the provinces.

Modifications and improvements have followed, but the essential role of the air-horn has remained largely unchanged. There is no telling what the future may bring, but there is little doubt that the all-electronic horn is a possibility. Perhaps one day the fully automatic train will sound out its warning with a computerised voice, making a sound which no old-time railroader would ever have thought of associating with a train.

Below: Imposing horn cluster, using Swanson's M-5 air horn formula, fitted to a Southern Railway System E8 locomotive. D. H. ELLSWORTH

The Brighton Belle

The origin of the *Brighton Belle*, and of the Pullman car facilities in the south of England, dates back to the former London, Brighton & South Coast Railway. The LBSCR was not the first railway to introduce Pullman travel to Britain, for in 1872 the Midland Railway's general manager had inspected George Mortimer Pullman's luxury cars in the United States and ordered several for his own company. By 1874 the Midland Railway had fourteen Pullman cars in service, and the London, Brighton & South Coast acquired its first the following year.

Strangely, that car was a sleeper, and not a 'drawing-room' or 'parlour' car, and, as no journeys on the limited LBSCR system involved night travel, it remained permanently arranged for day use. In 1884 it was sold to an Italian railway to serve its proper use as a sleeper. In 1877 seven new parlour cars had been added to the LBSCR service between Victoria and Brighton. By 1888 the first Brighton Pullman train was in service. Passengers could move freely from one car to another, and the whole train was lit by electricity – at a time when many homes in the country still had only oil or candle light.

In 1898 a new all-Pullman Victoria to Brighton train took to the rails, and outraged some public opinion with a Sunday service. By 1908 the Brighton-Pullman service began to run on weekdays as well as Sundays with the new title *Southern Belle*. Service was still limited to first-class passengers only, and as train-loadings became heavier, more powerful steam engines were introduced. The famous King Arthur class 4-6-0s and the Atlantics were the last steam locos to head the *Southern Belle*, for by the end of 1932 electric conductor rails had reached Brighton from London.

On 1 January 1933, a brand-new all-electric *Southern Belle* stood proudly at the platform at Victoria. The train included the first and only motor-propelled Pullman cars ever built. Each set had driving cabs at both ends, capable of producing 1,800 horsepower. The new *Belle* demonstrated its speed by covering the 50.9 miles from Victoria to Brighton in under forty-seven minutes, but even more impressive was the lavish interior design of the Pullman coaches, including its own electric ventilation system.

Following the disruptions of the Second World War, the *Brighton Belle* continued its service for some years, but the cars were becoming old. Under the management of British Railways it was decided that the expense of replacing the Pullmans

Facing page: Down 'Brighton Belle' crossing Balcombe viaduct in April 1972. J. BRADSHAW

Top, left: At Brighton in the summer of 1967. P. J. BARTLETT

Left: Cab of the unique Pullman five-car electric sets used on the 'Brighton Belle' service. P. J. BARTLETT

Above, top: One of the second-class motor coaches, part of the aggregate 1,800hp in a five-car set. P. J. BARTLETT

Above: A first-class coach repainted in standard BR livery. B. W. MOUAT

would be too great. Above all, the cost of maintaining staff was tremendous, and few meals were served on the short-distance journey, so that even with supplementary Pullman fares, the *Belle* was losing a good deal of money.

On 30 April 1972, the *Brighton Belle* arrived in Brighton for the last time. But not, fortunately, to be broken up. British Railways decided that the cars were far too famous, and sold them to private companies throughout the country, by whom they are now employed as bars, restaurants and reception centres. So after covering its course for more than thirty-nine years, the *Brighton Belle* will not be forgotten for many years to come.

The Great Western Railway

Of the four British railway companies to emerge from the Grouping of 1923, the Great Western was unique. It was the only line to absorb others, to keep its own territories and networks, and to retain its original identity. It took in thirty-two smaller railway companies, including almost all the Welsh railways and the whole of the railway-owned docks in South Wales. At the time of the Grouping, the GWR had 8,000 miles of track, 1,500 stations and halts and over 3,900 locomotives.

A great deal has been said and written about the 'Great Western Tradition', and it is true that over the years the Great Western Railway developed a personality of its own. Everything about it was different, including the gauge it used. This was the seven-foot gauge recommended by the company's first great engineer, Isambard Kingdom Brunel. Although at that time George Stephenson was calling for one standard gauge to be used throughout the country, Brunel so convinced company directors of the superiority of his proposals that he won the day.

There were disadvantages attached to this decision, however, for the GWR soon found its rail links with other railways were very limited. In 1846, some eleven years after the adoption of the broad gauge by the GWR, a standard gauge was laid down by Act of Parliament, and this gradually took over on the GWR networks. There had been some great opportunities in the early days of the railway, and in 1837 Brunel had appointed a young man of twenty-one as his Locomotive Engineer – Daniel Gooch, who was to serve the company for fifty-two years, ending up as its chairman. By 1846 Gooch had designed and built at the new Swindon works a magnificent express engine suitably named the *Great Western*, which was to be the first of a class which ran throughout the broad-gauge era.

It was Gooch who steered the company through years of great change, and he helped to bring Brunel's dreams of the broad gauge to

reality – and almost completion. No standard-gauge engine of 1850 could approach those of the Great Western in speed, power or comfort. In spite of the success of their broad-gauge design, Gooch also realised that the financial future of the company depended very much on links with other railways. He remained convinced that the broad gauge was the better system, but common sense prevailed, and the broad gauge had disappeared by 1892.

By 1910 there were more changes in the air and the GWR began to undertake a huge modernisation plan. New lines were planned and built, many sections of line were laid straighter, and experiments and re-

Top: Isambard Kingdom Brunel, who engineered the GWR on the grand scale with a track gauge of 7ft 0¼in. SCIENCE MUSEUM, LONDON

Above: Having laid its track from the beginning in the 1830s to Brunel's broad gauge, the GWR had to start in the middle 1860s on the huge task of reducing it to the standard gauge of 4ft 8½in. Conversion was completed in 1892. IAN ALLAN LIBRARY

search were encouraged in the locomotive department. A new boiler design was produced which was extremely sound and could be standardised for widespread use. Earlier, a new arrangement of cylinders and valves was tried out, and in 1902 the first of the big 4-6-0 express engines was running.

Next began a scheme for replacing the various classes of older engines with modern locomotives of as few different types as possible. Between 1903 and 1911 nine new standard classes were constructed and put into

use. Following this period of expansion and modernisation, the Grouping of 1923 had little effect on the overall function of the GWR. A considerable number of engines were taken over from the Welsh lines, but the older and smaller classes were rapidly withdrawn. The more modern and efficient locomotives were given GWR standard boilers and boiler fittings and remained in service. The Midland & South Western Junction Railway, also absorbed by the GWR, had its locomotives treated in much the same way.

At this time the GWR had brought out the first of its Castle-class locomotives, and these were to prove so successful that other railway companies not only borrowed examples for testing, but based their own de-

Left: GWR 4-6-0 Castle class No 7029, 'Clun Castle', at Cricklewood in 1969 – a 1950 double-chimney type preserved by the Clun Castle Trust. M. POPE

Below: No 6000, GWR 4-6-0 King class 'King George V', seen here with Pullman coaches, restored to running order by the Bulmer's Cider company at Hereford. V. C. K. ALLEN

signs on many aspects of the Great Western's Castles. In 1927 the first King-class engine was completed, since a more powerful locomotive was needed to deal with the heaviest West of England and Birmingham trains.

At the time of building, the King was the most powerful locomotive in Britain. Both Castles and Kings were a splendid sight, decorated with the well-known GWR livery of green and polished brass.

The GWR was one of the first of Britain's railways to introduce a system of automatic train control, in 1905. The device was simple and effective, and was the forerunner of the method still used on British Railways. The main object was to give an audible warning to a driver when his train was approaching a signal in the 'on' position, and if this warning was disregarded the brakes were applied automatically, and the train came to a halt.

The Great Western was always renowned for fast running and as early as 1848 broad-gauge trains were scheduled over certain sections to average nearly 57 mph. Some of the famous named trains at this time included the *Flying Dutchman*, from Paddington to the South West, and the *Zulu*, which ran from Paddington to Exeter in four and a half hours. By 1904, the GWR services were reaching Plymouth non-stop from Paddington, with long stretches of the journey covered at over 60 mph.

Of all the Great Western expresses, two stand out – the *Cornish Riviera Limited* and the *Cheltenham Flyer*. The former left Paddington at 10.30

a.m. each day until 1972, when it was re-timed at 11.30. The 'Ten-Thirty Limited', as it was known on the railway, was one of Britain's most famous trains.

From the point of view of rail-works, the GWR had a number of unique and interesting items. The Severn tunnel, with its gigantic pumping engines, was the longest

underwater tunnel in the world, while Brunel's timber viaducts in Devon and Cornwall were magnificent, as were the Saltash bridge across the Tamar and a similar but smaller one over the river Wye at Chepstowe. Compared with some other railways, the Great Western owned few hotels and even fewer ships. Paddington had the Great Western Royal Hotel, and Plymouth served the Channel Islands by Great Western ships, but these did not form part of any large network of accommodation or shipping. Like the LNER, the company considered itself to be a 'royal' line, carrying the Crown – special royal funeral services were operated which started at Sandringham and ran to Windsor. Special plaques and headlamps were also kept for such sad occasions.

Part of the secret of its popularity, and a reason why the Great Western will be long remembered, was its superb handling of public relations, which led to its image with the public at large of reliability and efficiency. Its staff were always smartly dressed, and passengers felt that there was something very special about travelling on the GWR. The company also produced its own books of engine classes, names and numbers, books on its prestige services, such as *Ten-Thirty Limited*, *Cheltenham Flyer* and *Locos of the Royal Road*. These were sold for a shilling, and there were also superb jigsaw puzzles of its trains, engines and tourist resorts. Thick handbooks, called *Holiday Haunts*, were issued and provided a fascinating mass of information about the areas

served by the GWR.

The Great Western was successful and admired because everybody, from the chairman to the engine cleaners, cared.

Left, above: Brunel's Royal Albert Bridge and memorial at Saltash. R. C. H. NASH

Left, below: A painting of the 'Cornish Riviera', headed by No 6000 'King George V', commissioned from G. H. Davies by the 'Illustrated London News' in 1929.

Below: A famous William Dean Single, 4-2-2 'Achilles', a design which bridged the changeover from broad to standard gauge. BRITISH RAILWAYS BOARD

Bottom: Preserved Dean Goods 0-6-0 No 2516, representative of a numerous and successful GWR class, in the GWR Museum at Swindon. R. C. H. NASH

27

Dart Valley Railway

Above, left: Staverton Bridge station on the Dart Valley Railway which runs close to the River Dart in glorious country for 9 miles from the main line at Totnes to Buckfastleigh. J. BROADRIBB

Above, right: Interior of the DVR's 'Devon Belle' observation coach. J. M. BOYES

Below: A Swindon (Churchward) GWR 2-6-2T at Buckfastleigh in 1970. C. J. GAMMELL

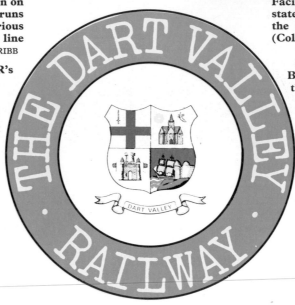

Facing page, above: Still in a decrepit state at Buckfastleigh after rescue from the scrapyard – No 1450, a Swindon (Collett) 1935 GWR 0-4-2T. A. D. DEAYTON

Facing page, below: At Staverton Bridge station – No. 6412, one of the well-known GWR 0-6-0 pannier tanks of the 64xx class built at Swindon (Collett) in 1934. J. R. ALLAN

The Flying Scotsman

One day in June 1862 a *Special Scotch Express* left King's Cross for Edinburgh at 10 a.m. That train soon became the *Flying Scotsman* (although the title was unofficial until after the grouping of railway companies in 1923) and became equally well known for its departure time of 10 a.m. which, except for a spell in the First World War, has remained unchanged to this day, more than 115 years later. The *Flying Scotsman* kept up another tradition until 1900 when, twenty-one years after the introduction of the first British restaurant cars, the passengers on the train could no longer stop at York and eat a hasty lunch before going on their way.

Two new trains appeared in 1900 which comprised American Pullman-type twelve-wheeled cars. Catering for all three passenger classes, the train-weight was considerably increased, but by then the first Ivatt Atlantics were beginning to take over from the famous Stirling 4-2-2s. The efficient North Eastern Class R 4-4-0s, later replaced by Atlantics, were also brought in, and problem of weight was overcome by the greater engine power.

The First World War interrupted the train's running between Edinburgh and King's Cross, but by 1923

Facing page: Locomotive No 4472 (later 60103) 'Flying Scotsman' just outside King's Cross, London. B. A. REEVES

This page:
Top: No 1 Stirling Single, with driving wheels over 8ft in diameter – one of the GNR express locomotives that helped to make the 'Flying Scotsman' famous. IAN ALLAN LIBRARY

Centre, left: A locomotive type that hauled the 'Flying Scotsman' north of York in the early years was the R4-4-0 of North Eastern Railway. IAN ALLAN LIBRARY

Centre, right: 'Flying Scotsman' behind BR Pacific No 60143 'Sir Walter Scott' in June 1951. R. E. VINCENT

Bottom, left: The restored 'Flying Scotsman', No 4472, then owned by Alan Pegler, that was in action on British Railways in 1967 and 1969. B. A. REEVES

Bottom, right: A 'Flying Scotsman' of May 1968 headed by English Electric Deltic No 9021 'Argyll and Sutherland Highlander'. G. S. COCKS

the service was back to normal, and the journey time had come down to eight and a quarter hours. Four years later another significant event took place. Because the owners of the *Flying Scotsman* and its rival the *Royal Scot* had agreed not to compete in beating each other's times, some other form of competition had to be implemented. Thus a long-distance non-stop run was made which easily broke all existing world records at the time. Since a single crew could not be expected to operate the train for such a long time without a rest, special corridor tenders were added so that another crew could take over by walking from their compartment to the footplate while the train was still travelling.

Later, more luxurious facilities were provided, including a cocktail bar, barber's shop and a special retiring-room for lady travellers.

Then, in 1932, the old agreement between the *Flying Scotsman* and the *Royal Scot* was laid aside and the journey times began to tumble month by month. However, the service was interrupted by the Second World War, and several years passed before the non-stop run was resumed. In 1955 the journey to Newcastle from King's Cross was made non-stop, and the train was reaching Edinburgh in seven hours.

In 1962 diesel power was installed in the form of 3,300 horsepower Deltic locomotives, the mightiest engines of their time, and the journey was being completed in six hours. Since then the time has been cut down even further, and, although some of the scheduled stops are longer than in the past, the maximum speeds reached have increased by a considerable amount, exceeding 100 mph regularly.

Far left, top: Alan Pegler's restored 'Flying Scotsman' surrounded by admirers; and far left, below: heading 'The Hadrian Flyer'. B. A. REEVES

Far left, below: The restored 'Flying Scotsman' heads 'The Hadrian Flyer'. B. A. REEVES

Left, above: 'The Flying Scotsman' in June 1969 on one of its appearances on British Railways before it went to the USA. The locomotive is now preserved privately at Market Overton. B. A. REEVES

Left, below: A Deltic heads the up 'Flying Scotsman' near Potters Bar in August 1964. G. S. COCKS

The London Midland and Scottish Railway

The London Midland and Scottish Railway was the largest of the four main-line companies to emerge from the Grouping of railways in Britain in 1923. Its chief constituents were the London & North Western Railway and Caledonian Railway, forming the West Coast route to Scotland, and the Midland Railway which, besides linking Leeds and Bristol, provided a rival trunk route to Scotland.

Other medium-sized lines thrown into the pot included the Highland Railway and the North Stafford Railway in the bustling smoky potteries. The LMS also acquired the London, Tilbury & Southend Railway which, logically, should have

gone to the London & North Eastern Railway. The LMS also shared joint ownership of two lines – the Midland and Great Northern, and the Somerset & Dorset. Besides this, it took over railways in Ireland, including the extensive Northern Counties Committee system and the Dundalk, Newry & Greenore Railway.

Of the English sections, the Liverpool & Manchester was perhaps the most important. It opened in 1830 as the world's first railway with all steam locomotive operation. The L & M joined with the Grand Junction Railway in 1845, and the pair linked with the Manchester & Birmingham and London & Birmingham in 1846 to form the London & North Western Railway. Another important part of the LMS was the Lancashire & Yorkshire Railway and the whole was a most impressive organisation.

When it was formed at the beginning of 1923, the London Midland and Scottish Railway had a total single-track length, including sidings, of almost 19,000 miles, and a main line 729 miles long from London to Wick. It acquired no less than 10,316 steam locomotives, of nearly 400 different designs, and it operated in 32 of the 40 English counties, (and until 1939, had a staff bigger than the British Army).

The progress of the LMS in the early years after formation followed a familiar pattern. Through economic necessity, a considerable amount of slimming-down was carried out, and many aspects of the railway's

Facing page, above: Euston Square station of the London & Birmingham Railway. SCIENCE MUSEUM, LONDON (B. SHARPE)

Facing page, below: A North Staffordshire Railway 2-4-0 passenger engine on the turntable. IAN ALLAN LIBRARY

Left: West Coast Pacific No 46200 'The Princess Royal' at Camden shed in 1962. M. POPE

Below: LMS No 6228 'Duchess of Rutland' on the down 'Midday Scot' at Kilburn, January 1962. L. KING

cylinder Royal Scot class were built. The first of these new engines emerged in 1927, and the series proved to be a reasonable stop-gap until William Stanier left the Great Western Railway to become the LMS

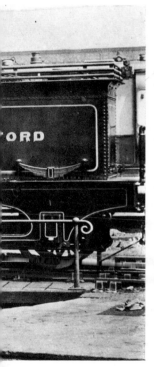

functioning were standardised. By 1930 unprofitable lines began to be closed down and, with the advance of road traffic, over thirty branches were closed to passenger traffic in the same year.

On the mechanical side, the huge collection of locomotives of varying age and efficiency led to complications. There were also big differences between operational practices in different sections of the new railway. The London & North Western, for example, thought nothing of attach-ing 450 tons behind one of its George V class 4-4-0s, whereas the Midland would have provided two such engines for the same load. Gradually, weak and non-standard engines went to the scrapyard, and, in the main, Midland designs were used for the replacements.

Soon the need arose for an LMS-built express engine suitable for the heavier trains. After trials and much study of other locomotives, such as the Lord Nelson class of the Southern Railway, fifty engines of the three-Chief Mechanical Engineer.

Stanier immediately began a programme of standardisation of both locomotives and rolling stock, introducing his own efficient designs and quickly cutting down the number of older locomotives. Among his famous classes were the Princess Royal and Coronation classes, the latter being some of the finest express engines to be designed and operated in Britain. Freight was worked generally by a large class of ex-LNWR 0-8-0s and Midland 0-6-0s of varying

power. Later, for freight work, Stanier brought in his well-known 8-F class 2-8-0 of which 600 were built, as they were ordered by the government for wartime service. Some ended their days in Palestine and Egypt – one was seen still working in Istanbul in 1966! – but most were eventually brought home.

The LMS operated an excellent service of suburban trains, and the process of nationalisation with modern engines was continued in this field too. In the years leading up to the Second World War some significant changes were made, partly on account of the poor economic state of the times, and also because of competition from the growing motor car industry. Diesel engines for shunting were introduced in 1934 and orders for more were placed the following year. Mechanical equipment was installed in the running sheds to improve the handling of coal

and ash; the 'mechanical horse' with its trailer was brought into use for railway road services, and over in Ireland petrol railcars were introduced on the jointly owned County Donegal Railway.

Freight revenue, especially from coal, was still good, but there was a never-ending battle to sustain passenger traffic. In 1936 the LMS conducted experimental runs with its Pacific *Princess Elizabeth* from Euston to Glasgow and back, and, by 1937, the *Coronation Scot* had been introduced complete with streamlined locomotive. Inter-city traffic, as it is now called, was speeded up and the improvements to schedules, particularly between London and Liverpool, and London and Manchester, were well publicised.

The London to Birmingham services, though loading to heavier trains, remained on the two-hour timing, originated by the old North

Western Railway, which was improved by no more than a few minutes until electrification of the route in 1967. Although the crack trains were the Scottish expresses, the Midland division did well enough for business passengers, and the trains were well filled. Average speeds were not high, being generally under 50 mph from start to stop. Holiday resorts in Lancashire, such as Blackpool, and in North Wales were very well served.

The LMS was a leader in the improvement of railway signals. Coloured light signalling was introduced, and the company was the first in Britain to concentrate on that aspect of safety for high-speed trains. Like its main competitors, the LMS invested in other means of transport, taking a considerable interest, for example, in the large Midland Red bus company and operating shipping routes mainly inherited from the London & North Western and Midland companies, sailing from Wales and Western Scotland to Ireland.

In Ireland the LMS took over the Belfast & Northern Counties Railway, changing its name to the Northern Counties Committee. This organisation, based in Belfast, was built to the standard Irish gauge of 5ft 3in, and served principal towns with a good express service from Belfast to Londonderry.

In the days of expansion the larger railway companies built hotels, and the LMS was no exception to the rule. Most of the London main-line termini and stations in the principal cities and towns had their own hotels which were held in high regard for high standards of comfort and spaciousness.

Later, during the Second World War, the LMS rebuilt the first of the Royal Scots and so turned a reasonable engine into probably one of the most successful and efficient 4-6-0s to have run on any railway in Britain.

The LMS emerged from the war with plans for the future, one of them being the changeover to diesel power, which were carried on into nationalisation. The company also provided the men who were to influence the remaining years of steam in Britain, and continued to make enlightened contributions to modern signalling and the systems that we know today.

Left: No 48448, one of Stanier's 8F 2-8-0s in February 1968. M. A. COLLINS

Right: LMS No 6201 'Princess Elizabeth' at Tyseley in 1969. P. B. WHITEHOUSE

Below: Midland Johnson three-cylinder compound of 1902, rebuilt by Fowler in 1914 and in service until 1951. Now at the National Railway Museum, York. J. ADAMS

Bottom: Midland Railway Kirtley 2-4-0 of 1866 which continued in service until 1947; at Leicester Museum. J. ADAMS

Severn Valley Railway

Near the centre of England, with headquarters in Shropshire, is one of the best-known railway preservation schemes in the country – the Severn Valley Railway. The original railway was opened to traffic in 1862, but made little profit. For some time the line remained a single track with passing loops at most stations. The increase in motor traffic on the roads severely affected the goods traffic, and eventually the transport of coal from Alveley Colliery to the power stations of Ironbridge, in the north, and Stourport, in the south, was the only important activity.

After the Second World War some of the steam engines were replaced with diesel railcars from the Great Western Railway, and when the GWR became British Railways' Western Region in 1948, operations continued only with a very restricted staff. In 1962 the line became part of the London Midland Region, but, an early victim of the closure programme of Dr Beeching, was closed the same year after 101 years of existence.

At this time of widespread closure of picturesque branch lines, and the removal from British Railways of all steam locomotives in the 1960s, rail-

way enthusiasts all over Britain were banding together to form societies devoted to the preservation of what remained of the old steam railways. One such group met at a public house in Kidderminster in 1965, and formed a Society to preserve the Severn Valley Railway. Two weeks later, urgent action had to be taken to stop the removal of the track at Bridgnorth.

A notable event in the society's

fortunes was the arrival of the first rolling stock – GWR 0-6-0 No 3205 and four coaches in March 1967. Since then a large collection of locomotives and rolling stock has been gathered together, including two class 0-6-0 tender locomotives, a Stanier Class 5 4-6-0 and an Ivatt Class 2 2-6-0, various ex-army machines and several more being repaired.

Although the Severn Valley Rail-

way does not possess the largest collection of steam locomotives in Britain, it does have the greatest number of passenger coaches. Some of them have been fully restored at Bewdley carriage depot, and painted chocolate and cream or crimson lake. One of the more interesting pieces is the engineers' breakdown train, which has its own working steam crane and accompanying match wagons. Diesel is also represented in the form of three shunting locomotives and one diesel railcar. The company, which replaced the society, is rightly proud of the results of long and painstaking work in restoring all its rolling stock.

Far left, above: Severn Valley's Fowler-built diesel-mechanical shunter No 17, 'Highflyer' at Bewdley in 1971. D. N. COOKE

Far left, below: General view of SVR's Bridgnorth station in 1972, showing the coal stock, a Peckett 0-4-0ST coaling crane, and Ivatt 2-6-0 locomotive No 46443 which was built at Crewe in 1950. D. N. COOKE

Above: Pure Great Western on the SVR as 1946 2251 class 0-6-0 No 3205 leaves Bridgnorth with a train for Hampton Loade in August 1970. A. G. BENDING

Left: Two industrial engines used for footplate rides in the yard – Manning Wardle 1926 0-6-0ST No 2047 'Warwickshire', that came from Portland Cement, Rugby; and Hunslet 0-6-0T No 686 'The Lady Armaghdale' built in 1898 that came from the Manchester Ship Canal via ICI. D. N. COOKE

Top: One of the Severn Valley's diesel vehicles, GWR railcar No 22 at Bridgnorth in 1971. A. G. BENDING

Above: Work on construction of a locomotive inspection pit at Bridgnorth in 1969. A. WILLIAMS

Top, right: LMS Stanier 2-8-0 No 8233 and L95 GWR 0-6-0PT, in London Transport livery, waiting to work evening trains in August 1971. D. N. COOKE

Centre, right: LMS Ivatt 2-6-0 No 46443 leaving Hampton Loade in August 1971. A. G. BENDING

Right: 'The Lady Armaghdale' blowing off in the Bridgnorth yard. A. G. BOWLES

Far right, top: BR 1954 Brighton-built standard class 4 2-6-4T No 80079 as received from the Barry scrapyard in June 1971. D. N. COOKE

Far right, below: Stanier Black Five Preservation Society's No 45110, 'RAF Biggin Hill', at Bridgnorth. J. HUNT

Golden Arrow

In the years leading up to the end of the last century there was fierce competition between the, one-time South-Eastern Railway and the London, Chatham & Dover Railway for the traffic between Great Britain and France. There was only one railway on the French side to provide access to Paris and beyond, and this was the Chemin de Fer du Nord, which put two ports, Calais and Boulogne, at the disposal of the cross-Channel steamers. On the English side the South-Eastern Railway also had the use of two ports, Dover and Folkestone, whereas the rival London, Chatham & Dover Railway had to confine its working to Dover. Thus it was that the joint services across the Channel between Dover and Calais were augmented by the SER services between Folkestone and Boulogne.

In 1929 a new service was started – the *Golden Arrow*. This service was restricted to first-class passengers only, had all-Pullman car trains on both sides of the Channel and a special first-class ship, *The Canterbury*, for the water crossing. On the French side, (after covering the 78 miles from Victoria to Dover in 98 minutes, and crossing the Channel in a further 75 minutes), passengers were transferred to the French *Flèche d'Or* (Golden Arrow) at Calais.

A Nord four-cylinder compound Pacific then took the train non-stop over the 184 miles to Paris Nord, which it reached six hours and thirty-five minutes after the departure from London. For the return journey, the *Flèche d'Or* was due away at 12 noon, and timed to reach Victoria at 6.35 p.m.

In May 1931, the number of Pullmans on the *Golden Arrow* service was reduced and ordinary first- and second-class corridor coaches were added to the service's facilities. The *Flèche d'Or* similarly acquired a second-class Pullman and sleeping cars. After the Second World War, the *Golden Arrow* service began again on 15 April 1946. The main train once again became a formation of Pullman cars only, ten in all, for both first- and second-class passengers.

Then, in the winter timetable of 1952-3, after pressure from the French authorities, it was decided that the south-bound *Golden-Arrow* should become the afternoon instead of the morning London-Paris service, and that the cross-Channel route should be from Folkestone to Calais. The original northbound 12.30 departure from Paris was resumed, and the steamer crossing on this part of the journey was to be made from Calais to Dover. Thus the service continued for many years with regular improvements in the times of the land journeys. The overall times, however, remained virtually unchanged, largely because of increased time spent in port.

The end came in 1972 when, on 1 October, the service was discontinued.

Above, left: No 34100 'Appledore', spick and span and decorated, ready for one of the last 'Golden Arrow' steam trains in June 1961. D. COBBE

Above: Battle of Britain Pacific No 34089, '602 Squadron', with the down 'Golden Arrow' near Tonbridge in June 1960. D. COBBE

Left: A 231G Pacific on the 'Flèche d'Or' at Port de Briques in August 1968. C. J. GAMMELL

Below: 'Flèche d'Or' double-headed by Pacific 231GK1 and 2-8-2 141R436, near Neufchatel in September 1968. C. J. GAMMELL

The Railways of Ireland

Below: Great Southern & Western Railway J15 class 0-6-0 No 186, built by Sharp Stewart in 1879, on an excursion near Listowel in June 1972. C. J. GAMMELL

The J15 class, whose design originated from Alexander McDonnell one of Ireland's best-known railway engineers, was one of the most numerous classes of engine in Ireland and was to be seen all over the Irish railway network. No 186 is preserved by the Irish Railway Preservation Society.

Bottom: No A58R, a GM-powered Metrovick diesel-electric locomotive, heading an express passenger train at Mallow in July 1968. R. C. FLEWITT

Right: UTA 2-6-4T on a goods train at Magheramorne in May 1967. R. C. FLEWITT

Below, right: From the Tralee & Dingle Railway; Coras Iompair Eireann (Cavan & Leitrim) 3ft-gauge No 3T locomotive at Ballyduff in July 1958. C. F. FIRMINGER

The 3ft-gauge was introduced when poorer parts of Ireland were opened up by light railways. Narrow gauge railways began to decline in the late 1930s, but the Tralee & Dingle, with its mountainous gradients and one-day-a-month operation stayed alive until 1953. The Cavan & Leitrim added engines from other lines to its own and continued to bring coal out of Arigna until March 1959.

How They Built London's Underground

In 1860 Londoners living near King's Cross were filled with wonder and admiration for a new and dramatic venture which had suddenly invaded their daily lives. This was the start of the building of the Metropolitan Railway, which was to become the first underground railway system in the world and, through the contraction of its name to Metro, was to give the world its noun for underground railways.

The original line was largely based on the ideas of Charles Pearson, who became London's City Solicitor. He drew up plans for a wide road, supported on arches, to stretch from King's Cross to Farringdon, and, below these arches, eight railway tracks running into a great City Terminus on both sides of Farringdon Street and linking up with King's Cross and Paddington main-line stations.

The Metropolitan Line ran from Paddington to Farringdon Street and at first had mixed-gauge tracks arranged as three rails combining the standard gauge of 4ft $8\frac{1}{2}$in and the GWR gauge of 7ft $0\frac{1}{4}$in. Thought was given to building special locomotives in a bid to cut down the smoke in the tunnels, but later it was decided to use ordinary engines fitted with a device to capture the exhaust steam and turn it back into water. Although, to put it mildly, the line must have been uncomfortably smoky, it became an immediate success, and soon after its opening in January 1863, more than 26,000 passengers were being carried every day.

The first part of the District Line, which came next, was designed and built by the 'cut-and-cover' method in much the same way as the Farringdon section to form a connection between South Kensington and Westminster. Meanwhile, the Metropolitan Line had built an extension which had needed deep cuttings and a long tunnel at Campden Hill. In the light of the simple engineering techniques used at the time, these projects were a remarkable achievement, and the obstacles overcome were considerable. The District Line,

for example, had to divert the West Bourne stream (which ran from Hampstead Hill to the Serpentine) over Sloane Square station in an aqueduct which can still be seen today.

Soon both lines were extended to Hammersmith, Richmond, Barking, Upminster and Watford. There was a time when the Metropolitan went out as far as Verney Junction, more than fifty miles from central London, and even ran Pullman cars on luxury trains to the Chilterns.

A road tunnel under the Thames was first proposed at the end of the eighteenth century. Initial attempts to build the tunnel proved unsuccessful as the river broke into the excavations, and work was abandoned until the invention of the tunnelling shield by Marc Brunel overcame the problems. Brunel's shield had twelve massive cast-iron frames, making up a rectangular box, and three compartments in which miners worked. As tunnelling progressed teams of brick-

layers moved in behind to build supporting walls.

The operation ran into financial difficulties and the tunnel, which was started in 1825, was not completed until 1843. Even then it never had its road approaches and remained nothing more than a footway until it was taken over by the East London Railway to become part of the London Underground network.

The Tower Subway Company was formed in 1868 to build a 'tube' tunnel under the Thames, and its Tower Subway, opened in 1870, had a few months of life as a railway. Passengers were taken down in lifts, hauled along the tunnel in a small cable-operated car, and taken up by lift again at the other end. The trip cost one penny – or twopence if you wanted to go to the head of the queue. The opening of the Tower Bridge, which was free of charge, near to the station virtually killed off all traffic.

The first Tube railway remaining in use as such today, although in modified and improved form, was the City & South London Railway, most of which now forms part of London Transport's Northern Line. After considering cable working, attention was turned to electrical motive power. A few small electric motors had been successfully tried out on other railways, and the directors of the line adopted the new method. The railway was opened to the public in December, 1890. From then on new lines were developed regularly and systematically. Under the guidance of an American backer, Charles Tyson Yerkes, the Bakerloo, Piccadilly and Northern Lines were started and the first two opened in 1906. In 1907 the 'Hampstead' tube, as the Piccadilly Line was known, was opened.

Gradually, the London Underground has been expanded to include several former suburban railway lines. The Victoria Line, the last section of which was opened by the Queen in 1969, is an example of the great advances that have been made in this field of railway engineering. Many of its tunnels are lined with cast iron or concrete segments expanded against the tunnel walls instead of being bolted together. The trains are driven automatically, and only one operator is needed to start

Left, above: Early aquatint of Baker Street station on the Metropolitan Railway. LONDON TRANSPORT EXECUTIVE

Left, below: Driving a tunnel under the Thames for the City & South London Railway. LONDON TRANSPORT EXECUTIVE

Top: London Transport's modern automatic-control trains of the Victoria Line at Northumberland Park depot. W. H. R. GOODWIN

Above: A London Transport train in the country but in direct connection with the underground network serving the capital. V. C. K. ALLEN

and stop the driving mechanism. The routes of all the trains are plotted and checked by computer. The bright and modern-looking stations have fully automatic equipment for collecting fares, and there is even a closed-circuit television built in to help deal with large crowds when necessary.

The Fleet Line, another new cross-London route, has linked the Underground directly with Heathrow Airport and, to the south, with the Strand. The most impressive aspect of the development of London's Underground railway is that it has overcome difficulties which few other railways have had to face, and has continued to expand steadily for nearly a hundred years.

The English Island Railways

The Isle of Wight was once the home of no less than eight railways, all of standard guage. The Cowes & Newport Railway, the first to become operative in June of 1862, was followed by the Isle of Wight Railway between Ryde and Shanklin two years later, and six more up to 1897. Eventually local amalgamation, or grouping, took place, and by 1914 three larger companies emerged. One was the Isle of Wight Railway, which operated in the east of the island from Ryde to Ventnor via Brading, Sandown and Shanklin. The second

ent until the general railway amalgamation in 1923 when it was finally joined to the other two island railways and taken over by the Southern Railway.

From 1923 until nationalisation of the railways in 1948 many improvements were made, but nothing was done that very much altered the character of the Isle of Wight lines. Then, in 1953, British Railways started to prune the Island's services and close sections of the railway until, in 1966, only the Ryde Pier Head to Shanklin line was left. This line was

engines were painted black, they were lined out in red and each bore polished brass nameplates. Other distinctive features were the sound of the Westinghouse air-brake pump and the unusual hooter or whistle. This was certainly a railway with a difference, and one which enjoyed great local pride.

Farther north, in what can sometimes be a tempestuous Irish Sea, is the Isle of Man which, as far as railways go, is even more individual in character than the Isle of Wight. The idea behind the Isle of Man

was the Isle of Wight Central Railway which ran from Cowes to Ventnor Town via Newport and Merston, and the third was the Freshwater, Yarmouth & Newport Railway, which remained independ-

electrified and operated by stock, still in its original colours, from the London Underground system.

Until the end, great efforts were made to keep the Island's steam trains smart and clean. Although the

Railway, which was registered in 1870, was to link up the four largest towns – Douglas, Ramsey, Peel and Castletown, with an extension to Port Erin. Later on, it was decided not to run the line as far as Ramsey,

Far left: Isle of Man Railway 2-4-0T No 10, 'G. H. Wood', with a Douglas-Ramsey train at Sulby Bridge in July 1968. G. DANIELS

Top, left: No 11, 'Maitland' waiting to leave Douglas in June 1972. J. ADAMS

Top, right: Fourth-rail electric stock from London Transport Underground, in its original livery, at Ryde Esplanade, en route for Pierhead, in 1969. G. M. KICHENSIDE

Above: O2 No 24 'Calbourne', preserved by the Wight Locomotive Society, in the Southern Railway 'sunshine' lettering style of the immediate pre-war years, at Havenstreet in September 1971. G. M. KICHENSIDE

but on 1 July 1873 the Douglas to Peel line was officially opened and public service began the following day. The Port Erin line was opened the next year on 1 August.

The north of the Island was not at all pleased that the Ramsey link had not been included in the plans of the Isle of Man Railway, and in 1879 the Manx Northern Railway Company opened the line from St John's Station on the Isle of Man Railway to Ramsey. A third railway was the St John's & Foxdale Railway, which was opened to traffic in 1886, and was operated by the Manx Northern Railway.

In all there were sixteen locomotives on the Isle of Man Railway, and all but one were 2-4-0Ts built by Beyer Peacock. The exception was an 0-6-0T built by Dübs & Co. All the engines are named and have copper-capped chimneys and polished brass domes. As supplied, the engines were painted a medium light green with red and white lining. After the Second World War they were re-painted a reddish brown, but later reverted to the original green.

Passenger traffic was good until 1956, when over a million passengers a year were still being carried, but from then on things went downhill. In the winter of 1964-5, only the Port Erin line was kept open, but this closed completely the following year. It appeared that the end had come. However, much went on behind the scenes and in June 1967, the line was re-opened under a new organisation with the Marquis of Ailsa as chairman, but this arrangement lasted only until 1970.

The Isle of Man has one of the most original steam railways in the world and there is no doubt that this could be made a great tourist attraction. With the very interesting Manx Electric Railway, the Snaefell Mountain Railway and the Douglas horse tram, it forms a museum of the history of rail transport.

Right: Formerly Manx Northern Railway No 4, Isle of Man Railway 0-6-0T No 15, 'Caledonia', preserved in MNR livery, at St John's in 1968. M. POPE

The Royal Scot

The *Royal Scot* and the *Flying Scotsman* (those are the names we shall use although neither was official until the 1920s) have been great rivals since the early days of express trains.

The two routes from London to Scotland, one by the East Coast and the other by the West Coast, were completed at roughly the same time and immediately became keen competitors for passenger traffic. In 1862 the *Flying Scotsman* (then called the *Special Scotch Express*) began its daily service on the East Coast route from King's Cross, which it left at 10 a.m., to Edinburgh, but there was already the *Royal Scot* (then known as the *Day Scotch Express*) leaving Euston – also at 10 a.m. – on the West Coast route for Glasgow and Edinburgh.

Sometimes the rivalry between the two trains has taken active form. When the exclusive *Flying Scotsman* was opened to *third-class* passengers in 1888, the West Coast companies countered by cutting the *Royal Scot*'s time from Euston to Edinburgh by an hour so that the train took exactly the same time as the *Flying Scotsman*.

The East Coast companies immediately cut the *Flying Scotsman*'s time by half an hour and started a battle which ended only when the *Flying Scotsman* travelled from King's Cross to Edinburgh in seven hours and twenty-seven minutes. Then, by common consent, the so-called Race to Edinburgh was called off and times to Edinburgh were fixed at eight and a quarter hours from King's Cross and eight and a half hours from Euston.

But this agreement did more harm than good by limiting progress on the routes, and the agreed times remained unchanged for forty-four years until May, 1932. By the summer of 1939 the down *Royal Scot* was covering the 299 miles to Carlisle Citadel station in an hour and a quarter less than in 1932, and arriving in Glasgow comfortably in a total time of seven hours. The up *Royal Scot* at this time ran non-stop from Carlisle to Euston throughout the year, and was the longest daily non-stop run in Britain for more than half of each year.

The Royal Scot 4-6-0 engines

would not have been able to cope with the much-improved times, but from 1933 onwards the far more powerful Stanier Pacifics, which were able to work their timetable with no difficulty, were introduced.

Not long after the Second World War, work began on the electrification of the main line from Euston to Crewe – a long and elaborate operation which took some years. In 1966 the *Royal Scot* proudly left Euston with a 3,500-horsepower electric locomotive, scheduled to cover the 158 miles to Crewe in 121 minutes at a start-to-stop average speed of 79.8 mph. For the first time a speed of 100 mph was needed for a train to keep to its time.

A still greater advance was yet to come. The London Midland and the Scottish Regions decided that from May 1970 new 2,700 diesels should be used in pairs. As a result, the *Royal Scot* found itself powered by 5,400 horsepower, and covered the 401½ miles from Euston to Glasgow in less than six hours, although there were stops at Crewe and Carlisle.

Since then times have been improved still further by full electrification of the line, and this has ensured that the *Royal Scot* has kept its prominent role in the field of express rail travel.

Facing page:
Top: Down 'Royal Scot', with 'Duchess of Hamilton' at the head, at Shap Wells in January 1960. COLOURVIEWS LTD

Second: Royal Scot class locomotive No 6100 in the condition in which it toured America in 1933. BRITISH RAILWAYS LMR

Third: A class 40 Co-Co 1 diesel-electric heads the 'Royal Scot'. M. POPE

Bottom: One of the original Stanier Coronation class streamlined Pacifics, No 6224 'Princess Alexandria', taking water. P. B. WHITEHOUSE

This page:
Top: 'City of London' hauling the up 'Royal Scot' at Hunton Bridge in June 1960. L. KING

Centre: A down 'Royal Scot' at Greenholme with EE class 40 1Co-Co1 No 236 at the head. D. CROSS

Bottom: Two EE class 50 diesel-electric locomotives heading a 'Midland Scot' train at Carron Bridge in September 1971. D. CROSS

The Keighley & Worth Valley Light Railway

The Keighley & Worth Valley Railway Act passed through Parliament, and the railway was incorporated, in 1862. Construction of the line began in 1864, but a number of difficulties arose, such as subsidence at Ingrow Tunnel which caused damage to a Methodist chapel near by, which delayed completion until 1867, when the final cost was £105,000 compared with the estimated £36,000. Although enough land was bought for a double track, only one line was put in. However, the company prospered until the 1920s, when the growing popularity of the internal combustion engine started a gradual but continuing decline in business until finally, on 30 December 1961, although 135,000 passengers had been carried during the past year, the last passenger train ran. Local opposition to the closure led to the formation of the Keighley & Worth Valley Railway Preservation Society and the reopening of the line under the Keighley & Worth Valley Light Railway Ltd in June 1968, since when the railway has gone from strength to strength.

Facing page: Two Black Fives, Nos 45212 and 5025, pictured running side by side on the KWVR in September 1970. R. LUSH

This page:
Top: Ex-Manchester Ship Canal's 0-6-0Ts Nos 67 (1919) and 31 (1903) between Haworth and Oxenhope in February 1971. R. LUSH

Centre: No 4744, a 1921 North British 0-6-2T formerly owned by GNR, LNER and BR between Haworth and Oxenhope in 1965 with a train of six vehicles newly acquired for work on the line. J. A. COX

Left: The 4-6-0 No 5025 again; this time on Mytholmes viaduct in September 1970. R. LUSH

Top row:

Far left: Gresley GNR 0-6-2T, later LNER class N2 No 4744, shunting at Hawarth yard in March 1970. R. LUSH

Left, centre: Removal of a Midland Railway signal box in connection with a new passing loop near Damems. R. GRIFFIN

Right, centre: KWVR diesel railbuses Nos 62 and 64 approaching Oxenhope station. R. S. GREENWOOD

Right: The Black Five No 5212 covered in wallpaper to prove the effectiveness of a Solvite adhesive. R. S. GREENWOOD

Far left, below: No 63, one of KWVR's WD 0-6-0ST engines, leaving Mytholmes tunnel in April 1970. R. LUSH

Left: Ex-US Army and SR American 0-6-0T No 72, hard at work on the KWVR in March 1972. R. LUSH

Below: Stanier LMS class 5 4-6-0 No 5025 at Oakworth in September 1970. R. LUSH

Travelling Post Offices

In the eighteenth century the British Post Office was bitterly opposed to a suggestion that stagecoaches should be used to speed the mails, but half a century later its controllers were more broadminded and within two months of the opening of the Liverpool & Manchester Railways, on 15 September 1830, letters were being carried by the trains. That was even before freight traffic began. By the time the Grand Junction Railway opened between Birmingham & Newton on 4 July 1837, the Post Office was able to offer a 16½-hour transit from London by stagecoach to Birmingham and thence by rail to either Liverpool or Manchester. A sorting carriage (a converted horsebox) ran from Birmingham to Liverpool from 6 January 1838, on the suggestion of Frederick Karstadt.

It was decided to provide a specially built vehicle for the service and John Ramsey (appointed Inspector-General of the Post Office for his idea) devised the apparatus for exchanging bags of mail at stations without stopping the train. The apparatus was incorporated in the new vehicle and used in conjunction with lineside catching nets and standards on which the bags to be collected could be hung.

Sir Rowland Hill, instigator of Post Office reform (including the universal penny post) was a member of the board of directors of the London, Brighton & South Coast Railway on its formation in 1846 and throughout his service with the Post Office (1846-1864) powerfully advocated maximum use of railway facilities for mail services. As a result travelling post offices became used to a larger extent on railways in Britain than anywhere else in the world. Not only is time saved by being able to sort letters in transit, but 'late fee' letters can be posted actually on the trains.

The parcels post was inaugurated in 1883 and two years later special Post Office parcels sorting vans were in service on the railways. At one time the requirements of HM Postmaster-General were said to dominate the compilation of the railway timetable, with meticulously observed exchange points, such as Tamworth, between the West Coast route and the Midland's south-west to north-east links. Although the Great Western, with the rather pompous phrase about 'compliance with directions received from Her Majesty's PMG', was first with exclusive night mail trains in 1840, the most famous night mail was the *West Coast Postal Limited*, which became all-mail in 1885, had some very high-speed running between stops, and was the subject of the famous documentary film which had the theme poem:

> This is the Night Mail crossing the Border
> Bringing the cheque and the postal order.

At the maximum there were nearly 200 TPO services and 132 apparatus stations on railways in Britain. The special services have been much reduced, owing to the development of the Inter-City regular-headway passenger network, road connections and air services. During 1971 the apparatus stations, which had been eliminated of recent years on many routes, vanished entirely, their ingenious techniques having outlived their usefulness.

Left: Trackside rig for mailbag exchange manned by Post Office staff, with bag ready for pick up. IAN ALLAN LIBRARY

Below: Preserved 1838 postal coach of the Grand Junction Railway. NATIONAL RAILWAY MUSEUM, YORK (B. SHARPE)

The Southern Railway

The history of the Southern Railway is closely linked with three local railways of the early 1800s. The Surrey Iron Railway of 1803 was the first public railway in the world; the Canterbury & Whitstable Railway of 1830 was the first to carry passengers by locomotive power; and the London & Greenwich of 1836 was the first railway to run into London. It is true, of course, that the Stockton & Darlington line was opened as early as 1825, but all of its passenger coaches were horse-drawn until 1833.

The main railway companies that came together to form the Southern in 1923 were the London & South Western, the London, Brighton & South Coast, the South Eastern, and the London, Chatham & Dover Railways – the last two of which had become the South Eastern and Chatham. Other lines to be drawn into the new organisation included those in the Isle of Wight, (the Freshwater, Yarmouth & Newport, the Isle of Wight and the Isle of Wight Central Railways). The Southern also shared the Somerset & Dorset with the London Midland and Scottish Railway, and there was also a delightful narrow-gauge line, the Lynton & Barnstaple, which was added under special powers of Parliament.

These railway companies between them covered almost all of southern England and spread well into the south-west. The largest of them was the London & South Western, which had a total route running line of over a thousand miles, of which 324 were single-track.

The Southern was very much a passenger line, dealing with vast numbers of commuters in the London area as well as holidaymakers and cross-Channel traffic. It spread its commuter network wider and wider, encouraging links to Margate, Ramsgate, Brighton and Sevenoaks. It advertised its seaside resorts from Kent to north Cornwall, and its cross-Channel services were intensively operated. There was also a service to the Channel Islands, and Southampton Docks were built up into the giant Ocean Terminal, which rivalled and then overshadowed Liverpool as the centre for the Atlantic passenger trade.

The Southern Railway's expresses, apart from those serving Devon and Cornwall, operated over comparatively short distances. The South Eastern & Chatham's termini at Charing Cross and Cannon Street were the departure points for the Kent Coast trains and the South Eastern's route to Hastings. Victoria served the lines to Brighton, Newhaven and Eastbourne, and trains from Waterloo ran to Southampton, Bournemouth, Salisbury, Exeter, north Devon and north Cornwall. Portsmouth and Isle of Wight trains ran from both Waterloo and Victoria. Pullman cars ran regularly on the *Golden Arrow*, *Southern Belle* and *Atlantic Coast Express* – the last being the Southern's longest express journey.

Barnstaple was the junction for the railway to Lynton, which was closed by the Southern in 1935, but which

Below: LBSCR Marsh H1 class Atlantic at Victoria station in 1908. A. WOOD

Bottom: Wainwright SECR 0-6-0 No 592 at Sheffield Park on the Bluebell Line awaiting attention. C. J. GAMMELL

offered one of the most delightful journeys that could be made. If it had survived the Second World War, there is little doubt that it could have become one of Britain's finest tourist railways. The Southern retained the Isle of Wight lines, and the train service from Ryde to Shanklin and Ventnor was as busy in the summer as a single line could be. By the early 1930s most of the old Isle of Wight companies' engines had gone and the traffic was worked by tank engines brought in from the mainland.

Electrification of the Southern suburban lines made considerable progress immediately after the Grouping of 1923. The London & South Western had already carried out an electrification project in 1915, following the lead set by the London,

Brighton & South Coast Railway, which had put in an overhead electric system as early as 1905, and had in all about sixty-two miles of electrified track out to Crystal Palace and West Norwood.

In 1925 the famous King Arthur class of locomotive was born at Eastleigh works and became an immediate success. This was perhaps the best-known Southern Railway class and, until their final withdrawal almost forty years later, King Arthurs were used on express services. During their time they hauled virtually every important Southern train, including the Continental services, the *Atlantic Coast Express* and the *Southern Belle*. Between 1926 and 1929 an even more powerful 4-6-0 class was tried out – the Lord Nelson, which

was a four-cylinder design. When originally built, the Lord Nelson was the most powerful locomotive in the country, and drawings of it were borrowed by the LMS when the famous Royal Scot class was being planned. In 1930 the Schools class was produced, and this was the most powerful 4-4-0 in Europe at the time.

Partly because of Southern's determination to electrify, and partly because existing locomotives were still able to perform their duties on secondary services, a large number of old engines lasted well into the nationalisation of the railways in 1948. Two ancient London & South Western classes had particularly long lives – the old Beattie 2-4-0 well tanks, and the Adams 4-4-2 tanks. Other classes working almost to the

end of steam railways included the N15 class 4-6-0s, the 02 0-4-4 tanks on the Isle of Wight, and the Maunsell Moguls.

Like its competitors, the Southern

Far left, above: Bulleid SR Merchant Navy class No 35028 'Clan Line' on a Waterloo-Salisbury train in June 1967. C. J. GAMMELL

Far left, below: Adams LSWR O2 class 0-4-4T No W26 'Whitewell' on the drawbridge at Newport, Isle of Wight. M. J. ESAU

Right: Electric mu 'Brighton Belle' unusually at London Bridge in April 1969 because of engineering work at Battersea outside Victoria station. C. J. GAMMELL

Below: Schools class No 30917 'Ardingly' heading a passenger train at St Mary Cray on the London-Ramsgate line. D. CROSS

was a company owning ships and docks. The ships were cross-Channel steamers (some owned jointly with French Railways), and included two larger vessels, the *Dinard* and the *St Briac*, which were used for the over-night run between Southampton and St Malo. Other steamers operated between Weymouth or Southampton and the Channel Islands, from Dover to Ostend, and from Gravesend to Rotterdam. In 1939 the Southern introduced a new ship, *Invicta*, for the luxury *Golden Arrow* service from London to Paris. Sadly, no fewer than twelve of the Southern's ships became casualties of the Second World War.

Of all its docks, Southampton was the most valuable and certainly the most famous, having the remarkable feature of a double high tide. Started originally by the London & South Western Railway, these docks were developed by the Southern into the country's main departure-point for Atlantic crossings. Other docks own-ed by the company included Dover, Folkestone and Newhaven for the Channel crossings, and the pier serving Ryde and the Isle of Wight. In general, the Southern system was very badly affected by the Second World War, as large stretches of its coastal holiday areas were prohibited zones. Its lines and depots were not only a target for aircraft, buzz-bombs and rockets, but the Dover district also suffered frequent long-range shelling. Nevertheless, enormous tasks were undertaken by the railway during the historic war-time retreat from Dunkirk, and in the gathering of the armies that were to invade Normandy in 1944.

Following the end of the war, some cross-Channel services were swiftly restored, and the *Golden Arrow* ser-vice was re-opened with Pullman restaurant cars back in some trains. Before long, the Southern turned its attention again towards leisure and holiday traffic, and at the same time plans were made for electrification to be developed further. The Southern helped to develop services in the outskirts of London and, like the Underground, its suburban trains be-came an essential part of daily traffic in and out of London.

Besides these commuter electrics, there were also the easy-going hop-pickers' trains, ramblers' trains, race-

goers' trains, and even opera trains to Glyndebourne, that catered for special outings. In time, however, the commuter services proved to be the most steady market besides the cross-Channel links. Perhaps the long-sighted, excellent planning that went into the extension of electrification has helped to prevent traffic con-gestion in and around London from becoming wholly unbearable. In this sense, the Southern has contributed to the well-being of travellers from all over the country who are not even using its facilities.

Top: Terrier No 32678 at Havant in August 1962. J. B. SNELL

Above: Southern Railway West Country Pacific No 34023, 'Blackmore Vale', seen here on the Longmoor military railway. The locomotive is owned by the Bulleid Preservation Society and housed on the Bluebell Railway. M. POPE

Facing page: Precedent class 'Hard-wicke' that ran between Crewe and Carlise; now preserved at York. J. ADAMS

The Races to the North-1888 & 1895

Vigorous competition broke out on the rail services between London and Edinburgh in 1888 and on the London-Aberdeen night services in 1895, the principal rivals being the East and West Coast routes.

The Great Northern Railway was partner in the East Coast services with the North Eastern Railway and used the lines of the North British to enter Edinburgh and Glasgow; the West Coast partners were the London & North Western and Caledonian Railways. The Great Northern, in November 1887, decided to admit third-class passengers to the 10 o'clock morning train from King's Cross to Edinburgh Waverley which had a nine hour running time. Third-class passengers were provided for on the best LNWR trains, but the running time was nine and three-quarters or ten hours.

The change shifted the balance of third-class traffic and once the LNWR and Caledonian were convinced that the shift was permanent they cut the time to nine hours on 2 June 1888. The East Coast reply was an eight-and-a-half-hour timing. When the West Coast operators announced that from 1 August their time would be eight and a half hours, the Great Northern replied with eight hours, mainly by running

separate Edinburgh and Glasgow portions. The GN relied on Stirling 4-2-2s and the North Eastern used Worsdell-van Borries 4-4-0 compounds which ran through to Edinburgh. On the West Coast, the Euston-Crewe section was handled by aged Lady of the Lake class 2-2-2s, with Precedent 2-4-0s from Crewe to Carlisle, and the Caledonian's 4-2-2 No 123, built in 1886, on the tough haul over Beattock to Edinburgh.

Final times were seven and three-quarter hours by both routes on paper, but the contest collapsed after the East Coast partners achieved seven hours thirty-two minutes for the 392.8-mile run, six minutes better than the West Coast companies.

The high averages of 1888 were far exceeded when the opening of the Forth Bridge gave a fifteen-minute advantage on night trains to Aberdeen for the East Coast party, to generate a new flare-up five years later. On 1 June 1895, the West Coast cut ten minutes from the schedule of the 8 p.m. from Euston, so that it arrived within five minutes of the East Coast train. On 1 July the East Coast group restored the status quo, so from 16 July the opposition timed the 8 p.m. to arrive in Aberdeen at 7 a.m. Early running by both sides led to hell-for-leather

operation of a token few coaches regardless of schedules, and then the signalman at Kinnaber Junction, whence both services used the Caledonian line to Aberdeen, really decided the contest each morning. The advertised East Coast time from 19 August was an arrival at 5.40 a.m.

On the last exciting night of the race the West Coast arrival at Aberdeen ticket platform was at 4.30 a.m. and the overall time for 540 miles from Euston was 512 minutes, or just on 63.3 mph. A three-cylinder Teutonic 2-4-0, *Adriatic*, got to Crewe at 64 mph, Precedent 2-4-0 *Hardwicke* went over Shap to Carlisle at 67 mph, a Drummond 6ft 6in 4-4-0 covered Carlisle to Perth at just over 60 mph, and a Lambic 4-4-0 thence right into Aberdeen, including the ticket platform stop, at over 66 mph. Often less than two minutes was taken for engine changes. On a typical East Coast night, Stirling 8-foot singles reached York from London at 62 mph despite a four-minute engine change at Grantham; Wilson Worsdell's 4-4-0s maintained 60 mph to Newcastle and 66 mph on to Edinburgh. There Matthew Holmes's 4-4-0s took over, to achieve 60.25 mph to Dundee and 56.25 mph to Aberdeen, 523 miles.

Railways in Scotland

Left: Workhorse of the Ayrshire coalfields, 2-6-0 No 42789 working coal empties at Falkland junction in November 1966. D. CROSS

Below: Two of the National Coal Board's Barclay 0-4-0STs shunting spoil trains in an Ayrshire coalfield in March 1972. D. CROSS

Right: Class 29 NBL diesel No 6107 with an Oban-Glasgow train at Crianlarich junction on the West Highland line in April 1967. D. CROSS

Right, centre: A4 No 60031 heading an excursion in April 1965, approaching Falahill summit on the Waverley route. D. CROSS

Right, bottom: A famous Scottish locomotive, the preserved Highland Jones Goods No 103 at Hurlford in June 1963. D. CROSS

Cornish Riviera Express

From the beginning of this century – and even earlier – the Great Western Railway took a lead in the length of non-stop running, not only in Great Britain, but in the world. As long ago as 1896, the GWR booked a summer express from Cornwall to cover the 193 miles from Exeter to Paddington without any intermediate stop. From July 1906, the GWR ran the *Cornish Riviera Limited*, an express service from Paddington to Penzance, in 6¾ hours.

Up to 1923 the Churchward 4-6-0 Stars had given fine service on the *Cornish Riviera Limited*, but with the load not generally exceeding 405 tons or so out of Paddington. In 1923 there had appeared on Great Western metals the first of a series of enlarged Star 4-6-0s – *Caerphilly Castle* – the first of a long line of some of the most capable 4-6-0s, which were to enable

the GWR to increase the weight of the *Cornish Riviera Limited* massively in comparison with other loads of the time.

The Second World War disturbed normal railway operations, but by the winter of 1952 the *Cornish Riviera*'s run was being completed from Paddington to Plymouth in 4 hours non-stop, but then diminishing traffic made a stop at Exeter desirable. For a time things ran smoothly, but a further decline took place in 1961 when, with a complete revision of the Western Region time-table, the train was booked to call at Taunton as well as Exeter in both directions. This meant an increase in the journey time from Paddington to Plymouth to 4¼ hours.

Between 1958 and 1960 the first Western Region 2,200 horsepower diesels had come in to displace steam

locomotives. These were followed in 1961 by the even more powerful 2,700 horsepower Western-class diesels. The way was now clear for an improvement in times never previously believed possible. By 1967 the *Cornish Riviera* was once again on a four-hour run from Plymouth, and that included stops at Taunton and Exeter – but better things were still to come.

In 1971 a bold decision was made to operate an hourly service between Paddington and the West of England. This meant that the *Cornish Riviera* could leave out the stop at Taunton, and, even with a stop at Exeter, would take no more than 3½ hours for the run from Paddington to Plymouth. That meant covering the 173½ miles from Paddington to Exeter in 140 minutes, at an average speed of 74.4 mph from start to stop, and a

maximum load of 300 tons, with a very slight stretching, allowed a nine-coach train. To keep the passenger total within reasonable limits, reservation of seats on the train became compulsory.

The *Cornish Riviera* is one of the Western Region's achievements that would have delighted the old Great Western.

Below, left: WR 4-6-0 No 5058 'Earl of Clancarty' arriving at Penzance with the 'Cornish Riviera' in September 1952. LESLIE OVERLAND LTD

Right: Inaugural run in 1959 behind the first Western Region 2,200hp diesel-hydraulic locomotive No D800 'Sir Brian Robertson'. BRITISH RAILWAYS WR

Right, centre: Warship D601 'Ark Royal' and the 'Cornish Riviera Limited' in June 1958. BRITISH RAILWAYS WR

Right, bottom: The 'Limited' headed by a WR 2,700hp Western class diesel-hydraulic on a viaduct somewhere in the West Country. BRITISH RAILWAYS WR

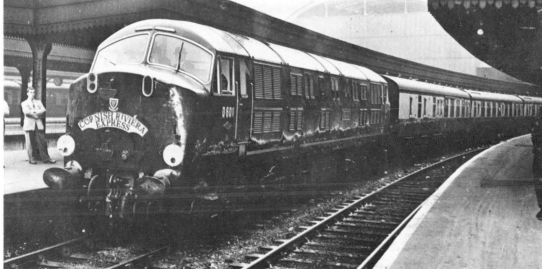

Level Crossings

There are more than two thousand public level crossings on British Railways and nearly four times as many private crossings provided for private use by landowners and industrialists who have to cross the railway. The need for level crossings was recognised early in railway history and rules were formed to protect both road and rail traffic at crossings. In 1839 the Railway Level Crossings Act required the railways to set up and maintain gates at level crossings of public roadways, and to employ a 'suitable person' to open and close them. The gates were to be kept permanently closed across the public road when not required to be opened for road traffic.

By the 1950s British Railways were finding difficulty in manning level crossings where there was no convenient signalbox for controlling the gates. The 'suitable person' of the 1839 Act was no longer easy to find, and the cost of finding employees to work the level crossings had risen sharply.

At that time experiments were being made with lifting barriers which were easier to operate by power and which would make the operation partially or wholly automatic. In 1956 a joint working party of the Ministry of Transport and British Railways visited various European countries to study their use of lifting barriers. Upon their return, members recommended that trials should be carried out at certain crossings using automatic and remote control of lifting barriers.

The particular form of half-barrier proposed involved a big change from the old-fashioned gates that the pub-

lic had been used to seeing. The gates used from the early days of railways had been designed to block the way to horse-drawn carts and other vehicles, and were quite effective in doing so. But if a motor car or lorry had failed to stop, they would have been of little practical use. The modern viewpoint was to regard the barrier as a warning rather than an obstruction.

The warning started as a train approached a crossing, with a series of flashing red lights; then, six to eight seconds later, the barriers were lowered. The barriers would be in position not less than eight seconds before the train reached the crossing. At the same time, an electric bell would ring to warn pedestrians.

The first automatic half-barrier crossing on British Railways was installed at Spath, near Uttoxeter, in 1961, and the number slowly increased. By the end of 1967, more than two hundred automatic half-barriers were in use, and the way was clear for a steady expansion. Then, on 6 January 1968, an accident occurred at Hixon level crossing in Staffordshire on the London Midland Region electrified main line from London to Manchester via Stoke-on-Trent, which changed the whole course of events and questioned the future of the automatic half-barrier crossing.

In the Hixon accident, a police escort car rode ahead of a huge, slowly-moving, 148-foot-long transporter carrying a 120-ton electric transformer and returned to warn the drivers of an obstruction in the road ahead. But, at the crossing, nobody involved thought of using the

telephone to find out if a train was due, and the transporter slowly moved across the tracks at about two miles an hour. While it was actually on the track, the warning lights began to flash, but it was impossible to move the enormous vehicle either forwards or back in time to avoid a collision. The 11.30 express from Manchester to London struck the transporter at an estimated speed of 75 mph. The impact flung the transformer aside and killed the three men on board the locomotive. Eight passengers on the train were killed and forty-eight were injured.

For the motorist, the most obvious change that has been made since the Hixon accident is that the red flashing lights are now preceded by a five-second warning period of amber lights. The minimum time from the start of the warning lights to the arrival of the train has been increased from 24 to 32 seconds, and an illuminated sign lights up if the barriers are to be kept down for another train.

Other new safety devices include the use of closed-circuit television, which is considered to have a promising future, although there are problems in providing adequate lighting for the cameras to work at night. The safe and economical working of level crossings in remote country places is another problem facing the railways.

The Talyllyn Railway

One of the Talyllyn Railway's most interesting steam locomotives is the No 3, *Sir Haydn*, which was named after Sir Henry Haydn Jones, the railway's general manager from 1911 until his death at the age of eighty-six in 1950. *Sir Haydn* is one of six steam locomotives in regular use on the six-and-a-half-mile line between Abergynolwyn and Towyn Wharf at Cardigan Bay.

An odd thing about this railway is its name. The line terminates more than three miles away from Talyllyn, and there is no record of any intention that it should continue to Talyllyn itself. When Sir Henry Haydn Jones died, the Bryn Eglwys quarries had already been closed for three years, and the railway and its stock were well run down. But

despite plans to scrap the railway, the Talyllyn Railway Preservation Society stepped in and successfully bid for the purchase of the railway's assets. Membership of the society and the public's interest in the railway have both grown rapidly.

The original steam locomotives, No 1 *Talyllyn* and No 2 *Dolgoch* were delivered from their Whitehaven builders in 1865-6, and are still in service. Both engines were in need of major attention when the society acquired the line. Two more locomotives were purchased from the nearby Corris Railway, which had been closed a few years earlier by British Railways. The new arrivals were named *Sir Haydn* and *Edward Thomas*, and have since been joined by further additions.

When the *Sir Haydn* was examined after its arrival early in 1951, it was found to be in a very poor condition after a long period of idleness. Despite this, it was steaming again by June of that year, though not in regular service because of the inadequate state of the track. In 1958, *Sir Haydn* was given new boilers and a complete overhaul, including replacement of the vacuum brake with a steam brake, to bring it into line with the remainder of the Talyllyn Railway's locomotives.

Below: No 1, 'Talyllyn', originally 0-4-0ST of 1864 converted to 0-4-2ST with original 1866 train at Brynglas. J. F. RIMMER

Overleaf: No 3, 'Sir Haydn', on the rehabilitated Talyllyn Railway. J. ADAMS

Top, left: No 4, 0-4-2ST 'Edward Thomas' of 1921, with No 1 at Wharf station in April 1968. J. ADAMS

Left: Fletcher, Jennings 0-4-0WT, No 2 'Dolgoch', and loaded train approaching Pendre in September 1968. J. ADAMS

Bottom, left: Towyn Wharf station in August 1970. J. ADAMS

Above: No 3, 'Sir Haydn', which came from the Corris Railway, crossing an ungated road near Brynglas station. J. F. RIMMER

Below: A train headed by No 4, 'Edward Thomas', gets the right-away from a volunteer guard at Dolgoch Falls station. J. F. RIMMER

Railway Ships

Railway Companies, said Parliament, should operate railway services and not own steamers, when in 1848 four railways sought permission to become shipowners, having previously relied on contractors or loosely related concerns. In fact, the required powers were granted to the Chester & Holyhead Railway on the grounds that the service to Ireland was the sole reason for a railway to Holyhead, and for a steamer connection to be operated by the Furness. The Brighton and the South Western companies were the other applicants; the Brighton proposal was turned down, and afterwards the company was reprimanded for attempting the task through a subsidiary; the LSWR was granted permission for fourteen years but did not exercise its rights.

The Chester & Holyhead powers were exercised by the London & North Western Railway. The next successful applicant was the South Eastern in 1853. In the 1860s there was a spate of grants – to London, Chatham & Dover and the London, Brighton & South Coast in 1862; the Great Eastern in 1863, and the Manchester, Sheffield & Lincolnshire to specified ports across the North Sea in 1864.

The Great Western obtained powers in 1871 and operation started the next year. Having been granted powers, the Lancashire & Yorkshire purchased the fleet of the North Lancashire Steam Navigation company jointly with the LNWR in 1873, and soon built up a big fleet on the North Sea. The Lancashire & Yorkshire eventually had the largest fleet of the pre-grouping companies, with twenty-eight ships wholly owned and seven joint with the LNWR. Lastcomer to the field of railway ship operators was the Midland Railway, which became interested after the purchase of the Belfast & Northern Counties Railway in 1903 and the opening of Heysham harbour the following year. To meet the requirements of the French postal service, some London, Chatham & Dover ships sailed for a time under the French flag.

The railway ships have maintained high standards of comfort, especially on overnight services such as Parkeston Quay to Hook of Holland; the LC & D made several experiments with double-hulled ships to mitigate the effects of rolling in the Channel and it was the Southern Railway which first applied the Denny-Brown stabiliser commercially, having built twenty-nine new ships in the first ten years of its existence. Previously, the South Eastern & Chatham had been among the first to order turbine-driven vessels, back in 1902. In 1938 the Southern Railway introduced a vessel with Voith-Schneider propellers on the Lymington-Yarmouth service which traverses a sinuous river estuary and where precise directional control is essential.

When the main-line railway companies were vested in the British Transport Commission in 1948, the fleet transferred included 122 ships totalling over 60,000 tons net. The business has been developed as the Shipping and International Services Division of British Railways Board, trading as Sealink; today, the Sealink fleet includes not only train ferries (developed by the Great Eastern Railway in 1922 for freight, and the SR in 1936 for through sleeping-car trains from London to Paris and Brussels since the war) but roll-on-roll-off car and lorry ferries, container ships, and passenger and vehicle hovercraft operated by an associate company with which tickets are inter-available.

Below: London, Chatham & Dover train and packets at Admiralty Pier, Dover. A. WOOD

Railway Workshops

Below: Diesel-electric power car of BR's 125mph train under construction in BRE works. BRITISH RAIL ENGINEERING

Right, top: Pouring molten metal into moulds at the steel foundry at Crewe. BRITISH TRANSPORT FILMS

Right, centre: BRE locomotive works at Swindon, with diesel engine testing house in the foreground. R. C. H. NASH

Right, bottom: Main carriage assembly lines at BRE's works at York. BRITISH TRANSPORT FILMS

Far right:
Top: A diesel railcar converted by BRE's Glasgow works for Lamco in Liberia. BRITISH TRANSPORT FILMS

Above, centre: Welding work on a coach being assembled in a turnover fixture. BRITISH TRANSPORT FILMS

Below, centre: Laying up a plastic roof panel at Derby by a machine which sprays glass fibre and resin simultaneously into the mould for curing. BRITISH TRANSPORT FILMS

Bottom: Container-crane grappler beams with press-button adjustment for handling different types and sizes of containers under construction at Doncaster. BRITISH TRANSPORT FILMS

Railways and Publicity

Even the first passenger service had to be made known to the public and ever since many different forms of publicity have been employed by railway companies. Posters, pamphlets, brochures, bookmarks, lantern slides, books and films have all played their parts in giving factual information about the services offered or changes in timetables; for prestige advertising; and in other peoples' advertisements that have appeared on the railways.

For factual information, the early railways simply followed the traditions of the stagecoach companies, issuing printed posters which were badly designed, clumsily produced, and generally not very effective. The Stockton & Darlington Railway's handbill of 19 September 1825, was a very modern-looking document·for its time, but few designers followed its example.

Keeping to the factual style of information, the Great Eastern Railway in 1887 issued a list of seaside and country hotels and furnished lodgings. The idea caught on and spread rapidly, but the promoters found it hard to resist using such long-winded titles as: *List of Lodgings at Seaside and Holiday Resorts, amid Hill and Dale in Wild Wales on the Cambrian Railways*. After reading the front cover, the eager holiday-maker was probably too tired to open the book!

In the early days the railways produced guides, timetables and postcards which were almost always sold at less than they had cost to produce, but with the development of cheaper printing processes, the pictorial poster soon came into widespread use. The great period of railway posters was between 1895 and 1914, and in those years attempts were made to publicise almost every aspect of railway trading as far as passengers were concerned.

At the beginning of this century the modest-sized Lancashire & Yorkshire Railway was spending

East Coast Types
No.5 The Deck-chair Man
Travel cheaply by L·N·E·R

SCARB

1932 BOOKLET FREE FRO
L·N·E·R INQUI

TAKE ME BY **THE FLYING SCOTSMAN**

LEAVES KING'S CROSS AT 10 A.M. EVERY WEEK-DAY

WITH APOLOGIES TO THE SOUTHERN RAILWAY

See a friend this weekend

There are many rail travel bargains—ask for full details.

Inter-City makes the going easy
(and the coming back)

Top:
Far left: An early example of 'knocking copy' by the LNER, with due apology to the Southern. NATIONAL RAILWAY MUSEUM, YORK

Left: Rail travel advertising brought up to date for BR's Inter-City services. BRITISH RAILWAYS BOARD

Bottom:
Far left: An LNER poster, drawn by Frank Newbold, depicting holiday resort characters. NATIONAL RAILWAY MUSEUM, YORK (B. SHARPE)

Centre: Another LNER promotion of one of the resorts served by its main lines. NATIONAL RAILWAY MUSEUM, YORK (B. SHARPE)

Right: A poster by Fred Taylor, commissioned for London Underground, to promote popular events in the capital. NATIONAL RAILWAY MUSEUM, YORK (B. SHARPE)

ROUGH

WN CLERK, TOWN HALL OR ANY FICE OR AGENCY

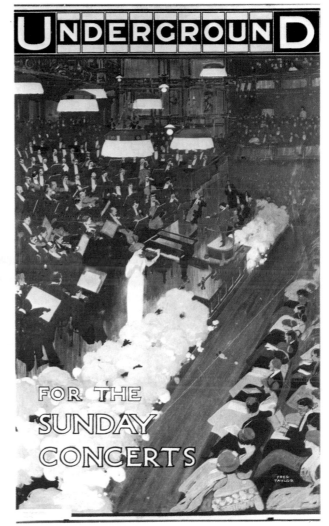

UNDERGROUND

FOR THE SUNDAY CONCERTS

about £7,000 a year on poster printing. But as the railways did not then use poster campaigns very much outside their own premises, they were appealing to members of the public who were already on the railway for some purpose.

The first signs of a modern intelligent advertising display came from the Great Eastern and Great Northern Railways. Against a vivid sketch of a windmill, the Great Eastern proclaimed *Norfolk Broads – Direct Route from Liverpool Street and St Pancras*. In 1904 the Great Northern, which had issued a long poster of an East Coast train much admired by railway enthusiasts the previous year,

reduced the wording of that to *Great Northern Railway* on a picture of a child paddling in the sea with his sister and mother. Other notable achievements became evident at about this time, including the well-known King's Cross poster in cartoon form depicting a jolly boatman skipping on the beach with the one slogan: *Skegness is so Bracing*.

Frank Pick was responsible for much of the raising of artistic standards in these posters, and he engaged the work of leading cartoonists and artists. By 1915 he had commissioned Edward Johnston, the leading lettering artist of the day, to design the Johnston typeface. This

is still used by London Transport.

One important factor in the selection of good poster designs was the part played by many resorts which were able to publicise their holiday facilities through the railways. Until 1911, however, only Blackpool Council was allowed to publicise at the ratepayers' expense in this way (although others followed later), and they even supported a shop in High Holborn, London, where the attractions of holidays on the Fylde Coast were displayed.

In the early years of this century, the third aspect of railway publicity – advertising of commercial products – was in use everywhere. Although

LMS   SP

BY SIR BERTR

many advertisers kept their slogans on railway stations reasonably short, some stations were so plastered with overlapping notices that it was difficult (as a District Railway traveller once complained) to 'tell whether one was at Victoria, Virol or Vinolia'. The London Underground began a clean-up campaign after electrification and soon not only established its own lead in devising posters, but pushed the Metropolitan into some splendid examples, such as the track scene beyond Rickmansworth, merely labelled *The Gateway to the Chilterns*.

Other railways followed the London examples and an orderly plan was developed by the trade advertising agent of the North Eastern, a former colleague of London's Frank Pick, in 1911. Under this scheme the spaces for commercial posters and those of the railway were set out neatly on every station on the line. All spaces were numbered and registered, so that there could be no doubt as to where the poster should be displayed. The advertising industry in the meantime had done much for commercial advertisers in improving the techniques of poster design and printing, and in time the poster came into its own as an effective means of transmitting information, rather than a cluttered attempt to catch the passing eye.

Far left, above: A Midland Railway poster commending the attractions of Blackpool. NATIONAL RAILWAY MUSEUM, YORK (B. SHARPE)

Far left, below: An announcement by two railways of special trains serving a non-railway event. NATIONAL RAILWAY MUSEUM, YORK (B. SHARPE)

Centre: 'Speed' by Sir Bertram Mackennal, one of the famous LMS advertisements commissioned from noted academicians. NATIONAL RAILWAY MUSEUM, YORK (B. SHARPE)

Below: A contribution by Fred Taylor to the centenary celebrated by LNER. NATIONAL RAILWAY MUSEUM, YORK (B. SHARPE)

Bottom: LNER poster advertising travel for one penny per mile, issued nearly a century after an Act of Parliament stipulated that fare for rail travel. NATIONAL RAILWAY MUSEUM, YORK (B. SHARPE)

L·N·E·R Our Centenary 1825-1925

"LOCOMOTION" driven by George Stephenson

ED

MACKENNAL. R.A.

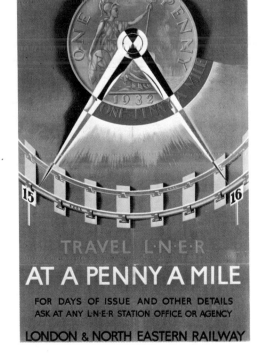

TRAVEL L·N·E·R
AT A PENNY A MILE
FOR DAYS OF ISSUE AND OTHER DETAILS
ASK AT ANY L·N·E·R STATION OFFICE OR AGENCY
LONDON & NORTH EASTERN RAILWAY

The Bluebell Line

The Bluebell Line is part of the railway which ran from Lewes to East Grinstead. It was opened in 1882, when it was meant to be a key secondary route between London and Brighton, but the traffic on the route never lived up to the promoters' expectations, and the line eventually became an antiquated byway, still geared to Victorian routine. The timetables remained unaltered and allowed lengthy stops at intermediate halts for picking up milk churns which were no longer there to be collected. Shortly before the final closure one passenger was led to remark that there was time to get out of the carriage and pick a bunch of bluebells without fear of missing the train, and the press of the time quickly coined the phrase 'the Bluebell Line'.

In June 1959 the old line was saved by a dedicated band of preservationists who acquired the property from British Railways, and by 1962 visitors were pouring in to see the fine collection of antique stock in operation. An operational start was made in 1960, although, because British Railways were still using the goods yard at Horsted Keynes at that time, the Bluebell Line had to terminate a quarter of a mile short of Horsted Keynes station and had no turnaround facilities.

Behind the groups which run the services there is a small nucleus of professional, paid staff in key positions, headed by a general manager or superintendent of the line. There is also a large and fluctuating number of volunteers who carry out casual work as ticket collectors, car-park attendants and bookstall salesmen. Not so obvious on a visit to the line are the many enthusiasts concerned with publicity who make an essential contribution to the venture's success, for there is a permanent need to produce posters, historical booklets, guidebooks and the Bluebell Society magazine *Bluebell News*. Others look after the enormous amount of correspondence that has to be gone into.

Towards the end of 1961, entry into Horsted Keynes station made true interchange possible once more, and the railway has never looked back. With each season, the crowds of visitors have increased. The number of coaches on the line has gone up steadily and includes several groups of coaches of similar design. The oldest set dates from the turn of the century and comprises four Ashbury ex-Metropolitan bogie carriages which arrived in 1961 and bore the brunt of the traffic in the early 1960s.

Membership of the Bluebell Society is more than just a formality. It entitles one to free travel and certain special facilities on the line, a copy of the society's quarterly journal, and participation in a host of social functions. Though the commercial steam age is rapidly becoming a memory, it is a matter of great encouragement to steam enthusiasts to see large numbers of young people joining in a railway venture of this kind.

Below: No 323 'Bluebell'; Ashford 0-6-0T of 1910 formerly SE&CR and BR (No 31323), now preserved by the Bluebell Railway. M. POPE

Right: At Horsted Keynes, the famous Brighton Terrier No 72 'Fenchurch' which completed a century of continuous active service in September 1972. M. J. ESAU

Right: No 488, an Adams 4-4-2T, formerly owned by L&SWR, and BR (No 30583), now in L&SWR 1918 livery. M. POPE

Below: No 27, 'Primrose', a Wainwright P class 0-6-0T restored to SE&CR livery. M. POPE

Facing page:
Top, left: Associated Portland Cement Manufacturer's gift to the Bluebell Line; the 1926 2-2-0WT 'The Blue Circle' with the ex-LNWR observation coach in 1964. G. D. KING

Top, right: Volunteer operating staff wearing Victorian costume to lend period realism to the scene. K. MARX

Below: Ex-GWR and BR (No 9017) 4-4-0; a hybrid mating of 19th-century Duke of Cornwall and 20th-century Bulldog classes, renumbered 3217 and named 'Earl of Berkeley'. M. J. ESAU

Last Years of British Steam

The steam traction which had served British public railways for 122 years up to 1947 was not suddenly cut off in mid-stream. It died a lingering and painful death over two decades. Between 1947 and 1950, hundreds of new steam locomotives came from the railway works and from the shops of private builders no longer engaged in the manufacture of war materials. Most of these new products were made to pre-1939 designs, and in fact engines were so badly required that types dating back to 1923 were built, such as the Great Western 4-6-0 Castle class, a few of which, constructed in the 1920s were being scrapped at Swindon before the new ones were fully erected at the same works in 1950.

Even after the formation of the nationalised British Railways on 1 January 1948, the shortage of motive power in any useful condition caused the need for over 400 engines a year to be constructed to cope with replacements alone. At the same time it was already clear that the tremendous advances made in engineering knowledge and techniques during the war would soon lead to the end of steam locomotives. As a result, nationalisation of the industry provided a valuable opportunity to bring about a major change. This opportunity was not only missed by those in charge: it was not even recognised.

There was no stark emergency. Three years passed between nationalisation and the steaming of the first British Railways locomotive to BR design. This time could have been more profitably spent in a close study of theories of diesel traction and diesel locomotives. The dozen new British Railways standard locomotive types that marked the last days of British steam were two classes of 4-6-2, two 4-6-0s, one 2-10-0, three 2-6-0s, one 2-6-4T and two 2-6-2Ts. In addition there was a single example of yet another 4-6-2. Of them all, the 55 Britannia Pacifics and the 251 heavy-freight 2-10-0s were the most successful.

Perhaps more marked than the new standard designs was the work carried out in rebuilding Group express engines, in particular the major reconstruction of Bulleid Pacifics and the modification of the Western Region Kings and Castles. The successful reconstruction of the Royal Scots, begun in 1943, was continued under British Railways until all seventy engines had been converted, and many other engines were modified, some more successfully than others.

From 1961, steam power began to disappear rapidly, but on no carefully thought out plan of regional conversion to diesel or electric traction, and with little control over the procedure. In 1968 the last steam locomotive disappeared from normal regular service. In the preceding ten years, something like 12,000 steam locomotives had been broken up in railway yards or by private scrap merchants: a sad change in fortune never imagined by British Railways steam locomotive enthusiasts who had welcomed the start of a new age on nationalisation day.

Facing page: Old Stanier 2-8-0 steam locomotive at Rose Grove Shed. R. BASTIN

Below: BR locomotives awaiting the breaker's torch. C. M. WHITEHOUSE

Top row:

First: 'Scots Guardsman', last of the LMS rebuilt Royal Scot class 4-6-0s, in traffic until 1965, preserved and finished in LMS livery. M. POPE

Second: GWR King class 4-6-0 'King George V', in BR livery at Bulmer's Cider Hereford premises; the bell is a souvenir of a visit to the USA in 1927. M. POPE

Third: 'Clun Castle', GWR Castle class 4-6-0 built in 1950 and withdrawn in 1965, now preserved by the Clun Castle Trust. M. POPE

Fourth: Reaching the end of the road at Ferry Hill shed, Aberdeen, in September 1966 – LNER A4 4-6-2 'Kingfisher'. P. B. WHITEHOUSE

Fifth: SR Merchant Navy class 4-6-2 'Clan Line', built originally with air-smoothed castings in 1948 and rebuilt as preserved in 1959. M. POPE

Below left, centre: Last of the BR

Britannia class 4-6-2s, 'Oliver Cromwell', now preserved at Bressingham Hall, Norfolk. M. POPE

Below left, bottom: Remains of BR class 8 4-6-2 'Duke of Gloucester' at Barry scrapyard in 1968. The missing

valve-gear is on display at the Science Museum, London. M. POPE

Below, right: The melancholy end of steam: discarded locomotives deserted and rusting while they await breaking up. C. M. WHITEHOUSE

Diesels Take Over

In less than sixty years diesel engines have taken over most of the world's railways that are not electrified. They have supplanted steam because of higher thermal efficiency, greater availability for work each day, greater cleanliness, possibilities of one-man operation, even of two or more coupled locomotives, and, in general, lower costs. As a typical example, with only 500 steam locomotives the Irish railways saved £1m a year on the fuel bill by turning over to diesel operation.

The compression-ignition engine has taken its name from Rudolf Diesel (1858-1913) although it owes much to the work of Ackroyd Stuart and Hornsby in Britain. It uses heavy oil which for many years was cheaper than other petroleum products and exhibits a much higher power transmission in the lower speed ranges than a petrol engine. Instead of a charge of vaporised liquid, the cylinder is charged with air, highly compressed. No spark is needed as the fuel, which has to be injected at extremely high pressure, is ignited by the heat of the compressed air.

Partly because the combustion chamber and bearings have to be robust to withstand heavier stresses than in a petrol engine, the result is an economic power plant capable of heavy slogging work. The change did not happen overnight. The first (Atlas) diesel-engined railcar ran on the Swedish Mellersta-Ostergotlands Railway in 1913; it had electric transmission and was reasonably successful but a bad reputation was given the diesel by an ill-timed endeavour by Diesel, with his old employer Sulzer, to build a direct-coupled machine.

In difficulty with boiler water on the Tashkent Railway, the Russians Lomonossoff and Lipetz adopted the diesel locomotive, with a government grant of £100,000, in 1922-24. They experimented with electric, mechanical, hydraulic and pneumatic transmissions, but were only successful with the first two; it fell to the Germans, twenty years later, to achieve lasting success with high-power diesels and hydraulic transmission.

First regular diesel services in the British Isles were on the 3ft-gauge County Donegal Railways with railcars. Although the Great Western was early in the field with diesel-mechanical railcars using bus engines in the 1930s, experience in Northern Ireland went into the British Transport Commission designs of the 'fifties. The LMSR perfected an 0-6-0 350hp diesel-electric shunter, but not until 1947 were fitful main-line locomotive experiments made and the late start cost BR dear after the 1955 decision to abolish steam. The change to diesels was completed with the withdrawal of the last steam locomotives on 11 August 1968.

In the Far East – in Thailand, for example – and in the USA, diesel traction was energetically promoted. The interest of General Motors in becoming involved in railways only partly accounts for this. The Ingersoll - Rand - GEC - Alco combination

was producing diesel-electric shunters in 1924 and Westinghouse Electric took out a licence for the Scottish-developed Beardmore engine, which had pump instead of air-blast injection.

In Germany the Flying Hamburger diesel-electric motor trains were running in 1932 and a great fillip was given to diesel traction in the USA by the railcar sets of the 'thirties such as the Burlington Zephyr, with schedules calling for averages over 80 mph and good maintenance records that helped sell the diesel to crusted steam locomotive engineers.

Above, right: BR class 47 diesel-electric No 1701 with a London-Sheffield train on the Erewash Valley line north of Nottingham in October 1970. V. BAMFORD

Right: No 63 'Royal Inniskilling Fusilier', a BR class 45, leaving Derby with a Sheffield-London train in October 1971. V. BAMFORD

Below: Four-unit-strong head end of a Union Pacific Domeliner train in the Columbia River gorge near Wyeth, Oregon. UNION PACIFIC RAILROAD

British Rail Today

Left: A Brush class 47 diesel-electric, bound for Paddington with a passenger train, near Bath. BRITISH TRANSPORT FILMS

Below: Arundel Castle, the seat of the Duke of Norfolk in Sussex, forms a backcloth to a SR 4CEP emu on the mid-Sussex line. BRITISH TRANSPORT FILMS

Right: General view of Euston station looking south towards London's West End. BRITISH RAILWAYS LMR

Left: BR electric locomotive at full blast on the LMR main line at Berkhamsted. BRITISH TRANSPORT FILMS

Right: LMR AM10 25kV electric mu at Crewe bound for Rugby in August 1968. R. B. HORNER

Far right: BR's experimental gas turbine advanced passenger train at the Derby Railway Technical Centre. BRITISH TRANSPORT FILMS

Below, left: SR 4VEP third-rail mu leaving Waterloo. BRITISH TRANSPORT FILMS

Below, right: SR 4SUB emu set forming a Victoria-Beckenham Junction train, at Crystal Palace in south-west London. B. STEPHENSON

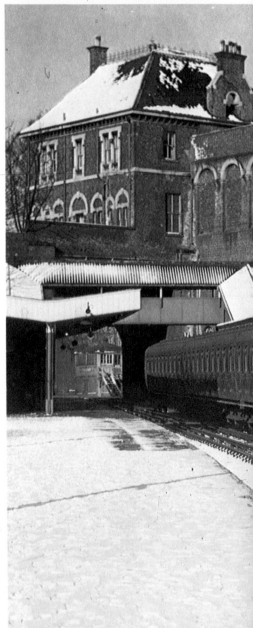

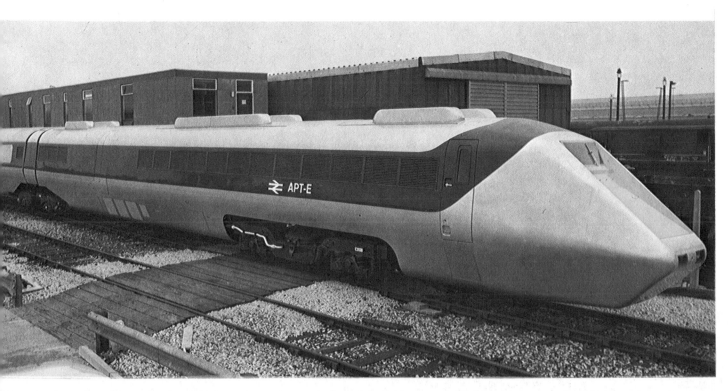

Top, left: A refurbished diesel mu train on a suburban service from London Paddington. BRITISH TRANSPORT FILMS

Top, right: The latest inner-suburban type of electric train, class 313, on the Eastern Region to work services between London Moorgate and Welwyn Garden City and Hertford North. BRITISH TRANSPORT FILMS

Left: West Coast main line electric locomotive on a train of modern air-braked wagons. BRITISH TRANSPORT FILMS

Above: Unusual combination of 2HAP and 4CIG dc electric mu sets forming a Victoria-Portsmouth train on the SR mid-Sussex line. BRITISH TRANSPORT FILMS

Left: One of the new class 56 3,250hp diesel-electric locomotives introduced to haul heavy freight trains including coal to power stations. BRITISH TRANSPORT FILMS

Bottom: One of the class 253 Inter-City 125 high-speed diesel trains which have revolutionised services between London Paddington, Bristol and South Wales. With a service maximum of 125mph they are the world's fastest diesel trains. BRITISH TRANSPORT FILMS